The Game Designer's Workbook

The Game Designer's Workbook

Hands-On Tools, Exercises, Walkthroughs,
and Resources for New Game Designers

Bobby Lockhart

Eric Lang

To our families.

About the Authors

Bobby Lockhart is an award-winning game designer with a background in filmmaking and computer science. His focus is on learning-games, which have spanned from early childhood numeracy to career training. He has also made many games for unconventional hardware, including the Osmo, VR headsets, and Alexa, as well as custom-built Alt.Ctrl devices, which have been exhibited around the globe. He is best known for games that teach programming, including Codemancer, Ozaria, and CodeCombat Worlds. He currently leads Important Little Games, a small freelance game design and development company. He is based in Chicago with his wife, Courtney, and his daughter, Sona.

Eric Lang is an award-winning game designer and art director at Field Day Lab, where he helps lead the creation of artful, story-driven learning games played by millions of players each year ranging from 4k to higher education. With a background in graphic design, web design, and writing, Eric focuses on designing narrative-rich, practice-based experiences that engage players through meaningful play. His work has earned recognition from Serious Play, Games for Change, and nominations for both a Peabody Award and a Unity Award. Eric has collaborated with groups like PBS, Harvard University, IEEE, and the National Science Foundation. He lives in Wisconsin with his wife, Sarah, and their children.

Acknowledgments

Bobby and Eric relied on many people to help make this book a success, and though mentioning them in an "Acknowledgments" section is not enough to repay them, it's the least we can do.

Bobby's first and greatest thanks go to his wife, Courtney Stepien, for tolerating and encouraging his scribblings and to his new daughter, Sona, for providing infinite smiles.

He's also very thankful to the people who did the earliest testing of exercises, including Rob Zubek at Northwestern University, David Antognoli at Columbia College Chicago, William Chyr at University of Chicago, Will Emigh at Indiana University, and Jared Bendis at the Cleveland Institute of Art.

For their advice in finding the right publisher, Bobby would like to thank Anna Anthropy and Jesse Schell, as well as Brad King.

Eric owes his greatest thanks to his wife, Sarah, for endless encouragement, honest opinions and patience, as well as his two daughters for brightening every corner of his life. He'd also like to thank Sarah and David Gagnon for their input, advice, and wisdom, as well as Emily Kurth for design input, and for playtesting our earliest drafts.

Together, Bobby and Eric would like to thank the whole team at Field Day Lab, led by David Gagnon and Sarah Gagnon, as well as Jennifer Scianna and her students at the University of Wisconsin– Madison.

Last but far from least, we thank our publishing partners at John Wiley & Sons. By order of appearance they are James Minatel, Brad Jones, Navin Vijayakumar, and Pete Gaughan.

Contents

Bonus Round 173

How To Use This Book.

The best way to learn game design is to make lots of games. That said, there are skills that contribute to a good game design that can be honed in isolation. This workbook is intended as a tool to help you practice those skills, either as part of a class, as a self-study, or as a way of distracting yourself from real life. Working through it will be valuable to you, whether you are a student, a working professional, or a hobbyist game designer.

You'll also find the exercises have been categorized into types. This was partly to help us make sure that there weren't too many similar exercises in a row but also to aid instructors in finding and assigning specific types of exercises. Each category has an icon, and the full list appears in the "Types of Exercises" section.

Choose Your Own Adventure

The exercises are grouped thematically into chapters, and by no means must you do them in order from beginning to end. You may find a type of exercise that speaks to you and want to do them all or a type that you dislike and skip each one. You may be assigned them by an instructor in whatever order makes sense for their syllabus, or you may want to close your eyes and flip pages to choose your next endeavor. All of these are valid approaches.
It is an oft-cited paradox that games are by definition playful, and yet seldom do we take anything more seriously. We hope that you will treat this workbook like a game in itself and have as much fun practicing the art of game design as we did making a framework for you to do so.

Though our professional experience is mostly in digital games, and a smattering of tabletop games, the universe of interactive arts is large, and we feel that the lessons and intuition you'll gain from these exercises will be of use across the whole space of playful interactivity. The following is a (doubtless incomplete) map of that space. If you're interested in working within any part of it, we believe this book will be worthwhile.

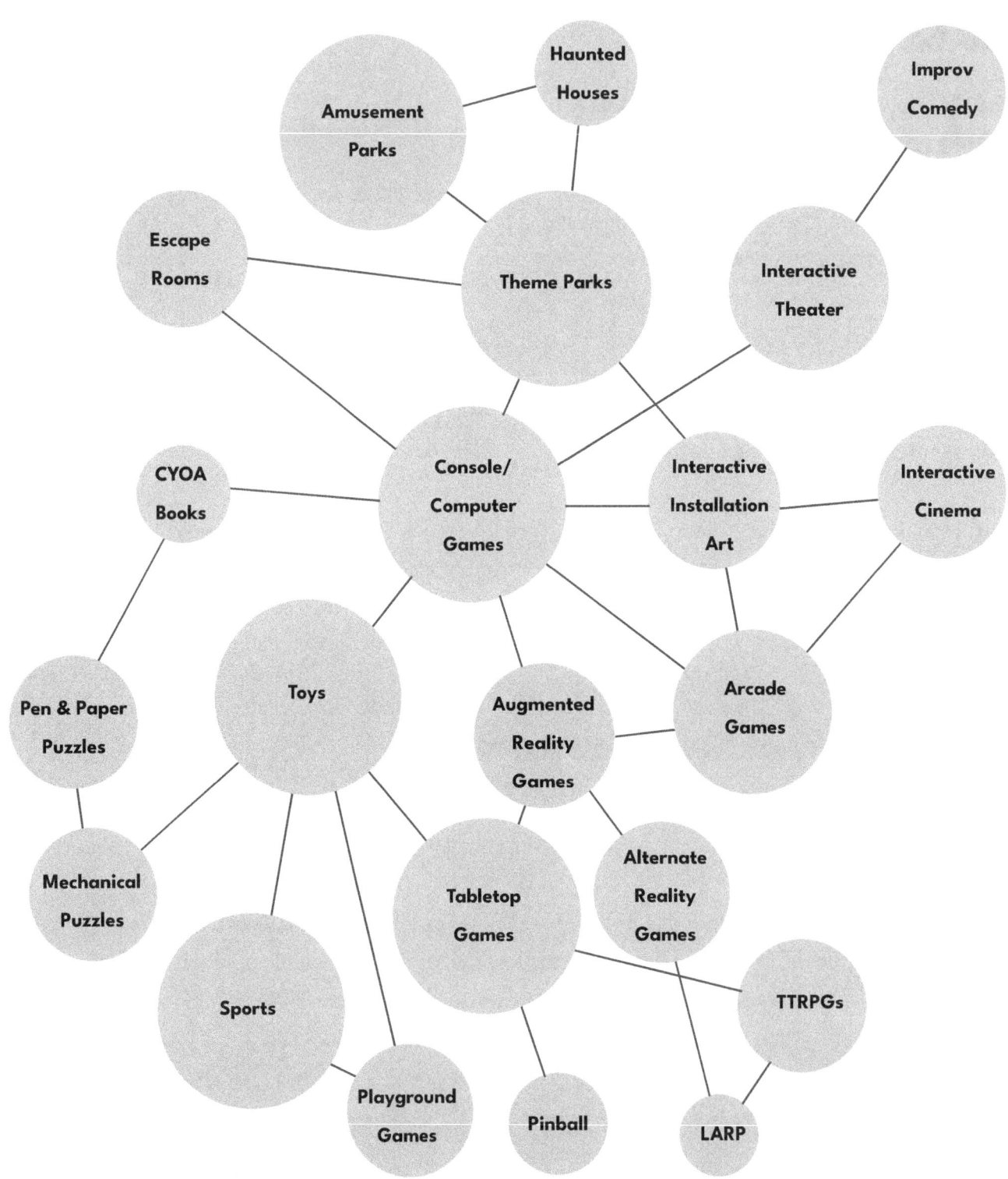

Types of Exercises

Reflection

These are mostly opportunities to process the lessons learned in other exercises and to think deeply about your future game design practice.

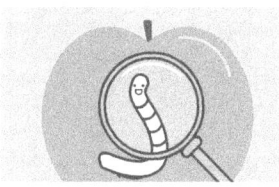

What Is...

These are meant to introduce a fundamental game design practice and to let you experience it firsthand.

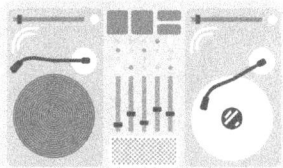

Remix

These challenges start from an existing game and ask you to modify and improve upon it.

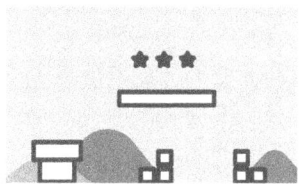

Level Design

These exercises regard the layout of elements within the space of the game's world.

Breaking It Down

Even the simplest games are composed of many, many interrelated parts. These exercises are designed to help you isolate and manipulate these parts.

What a Concept

These exercises introduce a concept that can be found across many games and task you to play around with it.

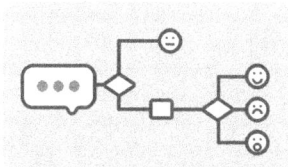

Narrative Design

Many people believe that game design is all about coming up with stories. It's not. However, coming up with stories can be part of the process.

Cross-Training

These exercises teach a skill from another discipline. This is something that, while not always part of typical game design, will make you a better designer overall.

Randomized Game Idea

As game designers, we are often asked to flesh out the details of a game design that was not our idea from the start. These exercises will force you to explore and to specify a design that is generated randomly.

Additional Resources

At the end of this book we've included more space for you to work in. If you need more space to complete an idea, please use it! Just remember to note what page your work is continued on. There are also some more random dice, cards, etc., in the back in case you need them.

If you're interested in learning more about a concept covered in a particular chapter, there's also a section at the end called "Further Reading." It points to other books and resources that cover the ideas we introduce here, but in more detail.

Lastly, you can go to **gamedesignersworkbook.com** to find more blank workbook pages, randomness generators, errata, a discussion forum, and even more resources.

It's ~~Dangerous~~ LESS THAN IDEAL to Go Alone.

Before you dive in, we just want to say that in our own lives we've found the process of game design more fun and more rewarding than any amount of game-playing could be. But like playing a game, the pastime is greatly improved by adding a multiplayer mode. For that reason, we recommend you find some like-minded others with whom to share the experience of this workbook. When you swap ideas and compare notes, the connections and inspirations you generate will delight and surprise you, and each of you will be elevated by the process.

Chapter One

Setting the Stage

———

The only way to learn is by playing. The only way to win is by learning. And the only way to begin is by beginning.

—Sam Reich
Game Changer

Reflection: Who Is the Game Designer You?

If you read through the introduction of this book, we wouldn't blame you one bit if you were daydreaming through some if it. Maybe you were imagining yourself in the future, accepting an award for your innovative game, or watching people line up outside an electronics store at midnight, each waiting for the chance to buy something you helped create. Well, that's what this reflection is all about. What do you dream of?

Specifically:

- What are your goals as a game designer?
- What kinds of games do you want to have a hand in creating?
- When your colleagues describe you, what kind of game designer do you want them to say you are?
- Is there something wrong about a particular genre of games, or about games in general, that you feel you need to correct?

TAKE THIS SPACE TO WRITE YOUR RESPONSES!

Throughout this workbook, we'll be asking you to revise your designs to make them better. Here is where you define what "better" means to you. Is it all about visceral pleasure? What about evoking emotion in the player? Self-expression? There are many valid answers, but it's important to define what the answer is to you.

Use this Space to define what "Better" means to you:

It's possible that over time what you value in a game may shift. It certainly has for us, more than once. The following space is reserved so that you can revisit this question and reflect on what may have influenced your change of heart.

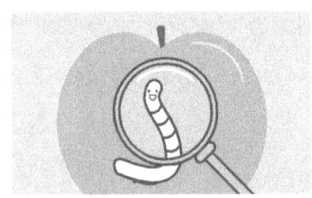

What Is...a GDD?

GDD stands for "game design document." In short, a GDD is to a game what a screenplay is to a movie. Though this book talks a lot about rules, rules are only part of what's specified in a GDD. A GDD can also describe the story and aesthetics of the game, how you want the player to feel, and more. Ideally, it should also have lots of pictures.

Rather than a single monolithic document, a GDD is often built of many smaller GDDs, each describing a piece of the game. One GDD might cover a game mechanic (aka gameplay feature), a level, or an non-player character (NPC) behavior. It's also a "living document," which is constantly altered over the course of a game's production.

The purpose of a GDD can vary depending on its audience and the stage of a project. Before a single playing card is scribbled into being or a single line of code is written, a GDD acts as a pitch, helping to sell the ideas of the game to external stakeholders, to members of your team, and to yourself. Once you start building, the GDD is the blueprint of the game.

TIME TO GIVE IT A SHOT!

Your task is to think of a game you know very well and fill out the GDD on the following page as if it were a game you were about to build yourself. Keep it general, describing the whole game concept at a low level of detail, knowing that more specifics will be fleshed out in future GDDs.

Since games are so incredibly diverse, **there is no single structure that GDDs take**, but we've created a form with some elements we recommend you include. It's not one-size-fits-all, so if a section doesn't apply, you can safely ignore it. If there is something vital about your chosen game that isn't covered, please add it.

Game Title

Executive Summary

Write one or two sentences explaining the basic idea of the game.

Audience

Who is the game for, primarily? There are a lot of ways to slice this. Demographics. Personality. You can also give examples of specific people who you think would enjoy the game, and why (we call these "personas").

Concept Drawings

Draw a couple of images representative of what the player will see in the most interesting parts of gameplay. In later chapters we will practice the kinds of visualizations that make a GDD come alive: storyboards, wireframes, and schematics.

Experience Pillars

What do you want the player(s) to experience, even if everything else about the design changes? What are the most important things you want a player to do, to see, or to feel?

Platform(s)

What kind of game pieces or computing hardware will the players be using?

Goals of the Player

Sometimes called the object of the game. How do players win? Can they win at all, or just do better than before? Is it the same for all players, or do different players have different goals?

Obstacles Blocking Those Goals

Other players? NPCs? The nature of the world?

Interface

Zoom out a bit. When a player uses their abilities, what are they actually doing with their bodies? Are they placing a card? Pressing a button? Swiping a touchscreen?

Story

Setting and Genre

When and where does it take place? What genre is it? It can be useful to refer to literature and film.

Main Characters

Include their name, whether they are playable or an NPC, a brief description, what they want, and what stands in their way.

Elements

What kinds of elements—objects, units, etc.—are players likely to encounter in this game? Just give two or three examples of what they are and how they operate to help or hinder the player. How do they relate to the other elements?

Remix: Tic-Tac-Toe (Naughts & Crosses)

Game designers often refer to the universe of possible rules, or rulespace, that they are exploring as they create a new game. This type of exploration usually begins using a known game as a sort of base camp. Eventually you may find the confidence to delve deep into the unknown wilderness of games to find the treasures that lurk there. In these Remix exercises you'll be asked to start simply, by charting the rulespace next door to one that is well-known.

The Rules of Tic-Tac-Toe:

1 Two players alternate turns.

2 Each player has a symbol associated with themself, traditionally, "X" and "O."

3 Play occurs on a discrete playfield of nine empty squares arranged 3x3.

4 On each player's turn they choose an unoccupied square and write their symbol in it.

5 The first player to arrange three of their own symbols in a line (vertically, horizontally, or diagonally) wins the game.

Your task: Try to improve the game of tic-tac-toe by revising one rule **other than rule 3**. Write your revised rule on the following lines, as well as which numbered rule it will replace. Be as specific as you can. Assume that the reader of the rule won't have you around to explain it.

TRY IT OUT!

Create your revised rule:

Try playing some games against yourself with your revised rule.

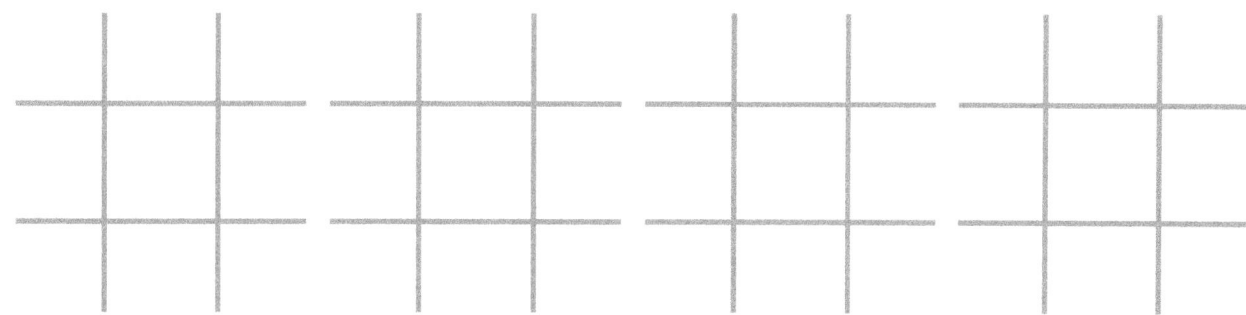

After some testing, do you think your revised rule could be improved? Write an improved version of your rule here:

Your RE-revised rule:

Try it out with your new and improved rule.

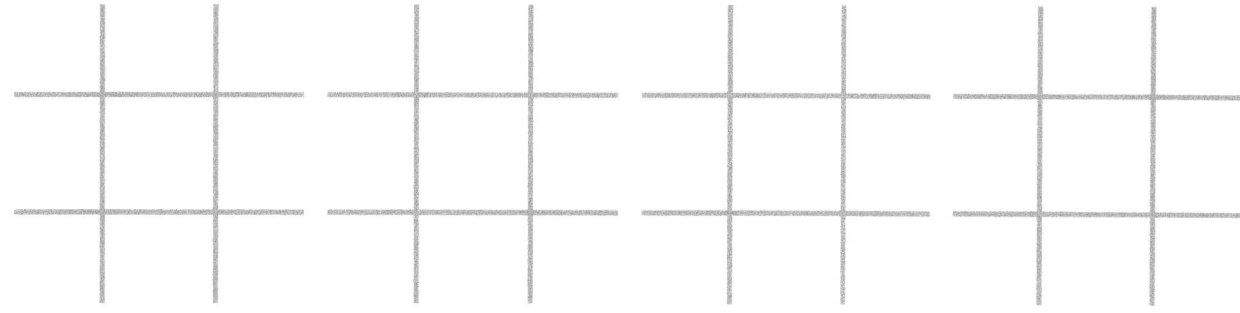

Tic-tac-toe is known to have a "dominant strategy." That is, a way to play that never loses. The dominant strategy in tic-tac-toe is to try to lure your opponent into a "fork." A fork is a situation where you have two winning moves and your opponent can prevent only one. (See the chapter "What a Concept: Forks" for more about that.)

Another attribute of tic-tac-toe that is widely considered a flaw is the significant advantage granted by taking the first turn. With your revised rule, do those problems persist?

Make any further changes to the rules you'd like to support your first rule change to address the first-player-advantage or negate the dominant strategy or just to try something totally new while keeping with the spirit of the original tic-tac-toe.

YOUR NEW RULE(S)

Try it out with your new and improved rule. Draw your own play areas in case there are changes.

Level Design: Mazes

What makes a maze interesting? You may have heard that you can always find your way out of a maze by keeping one hand on the wall. That's true for simple mazes with fully connected walls and exits on the outside edge, like this:

But it doesn't work on mazes like this:

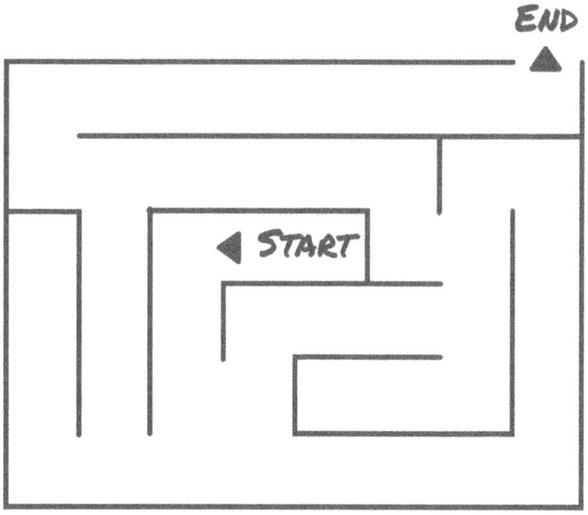

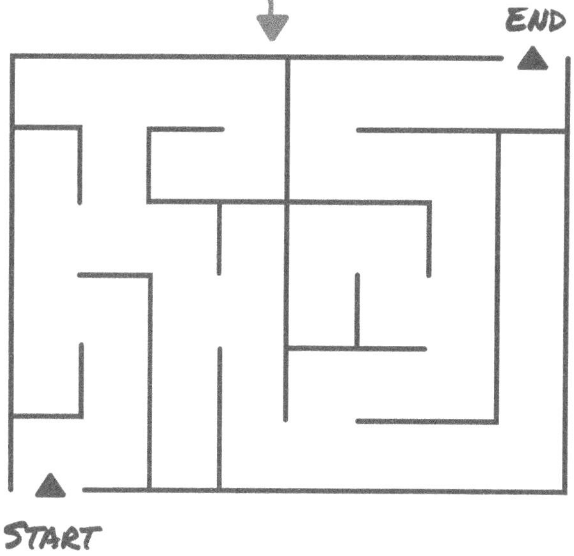

The right maze is harder to solve when you're looking down on it from above, but the left maze is more difficult when you're standing inside of it.

Try it Out!

Try making a couple of each kind of maze. First start with mazes that do not have "islands" in the middle. That is, ones that you can find your way out by holding your hand on the wall. Then try to make it more interesting by adding a floating section or sections. The endings have been placed. Choose your own starting point.

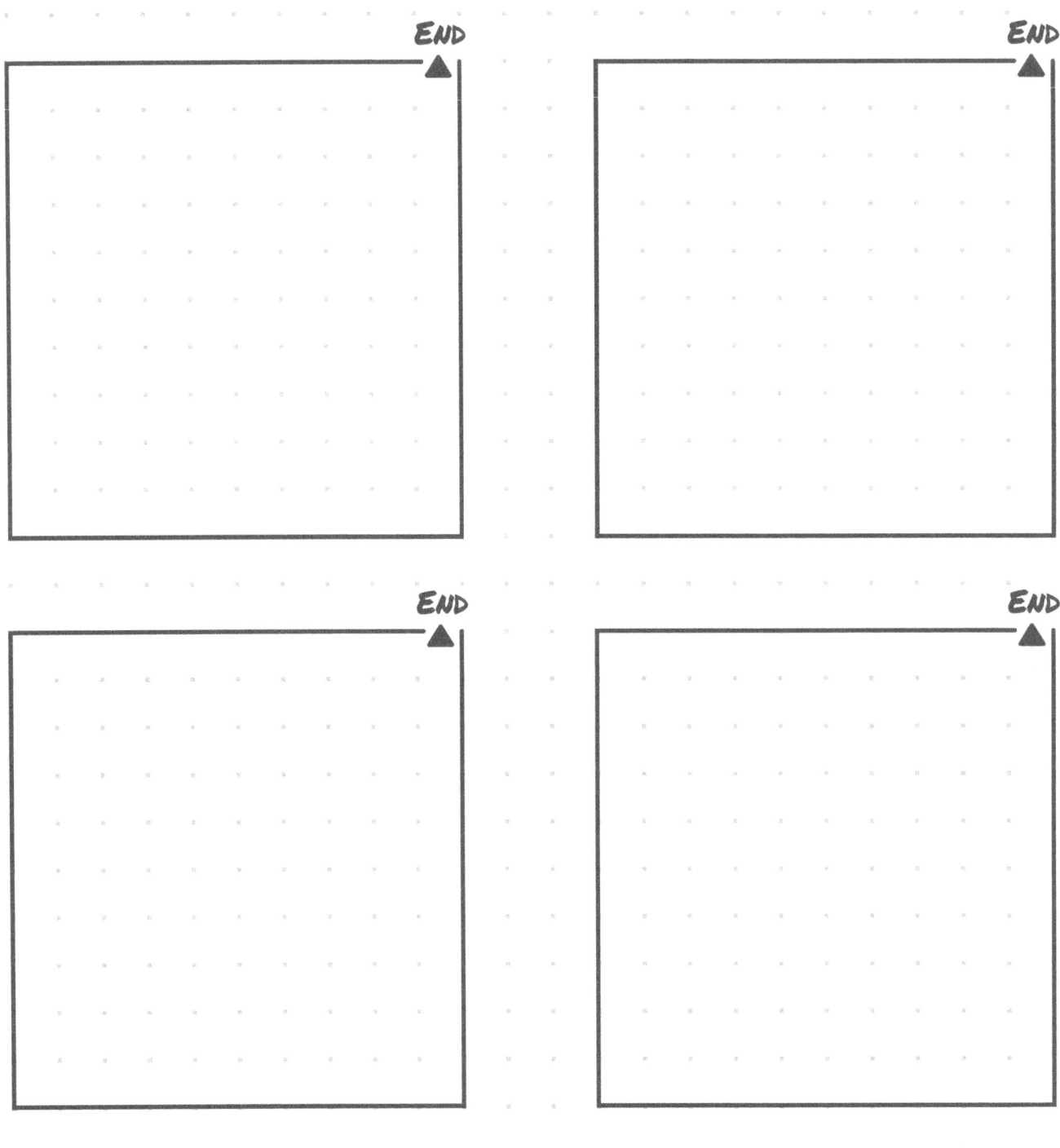

Non-planar Mazes

Mazes also get more difficult when they are non-planar, like this one. Solve this non-planar maze for yourself, drawing the path you take.

TRY IT OUT!

Try making some non-planar mazes here. The endings have been placed. Choose your own starting point.

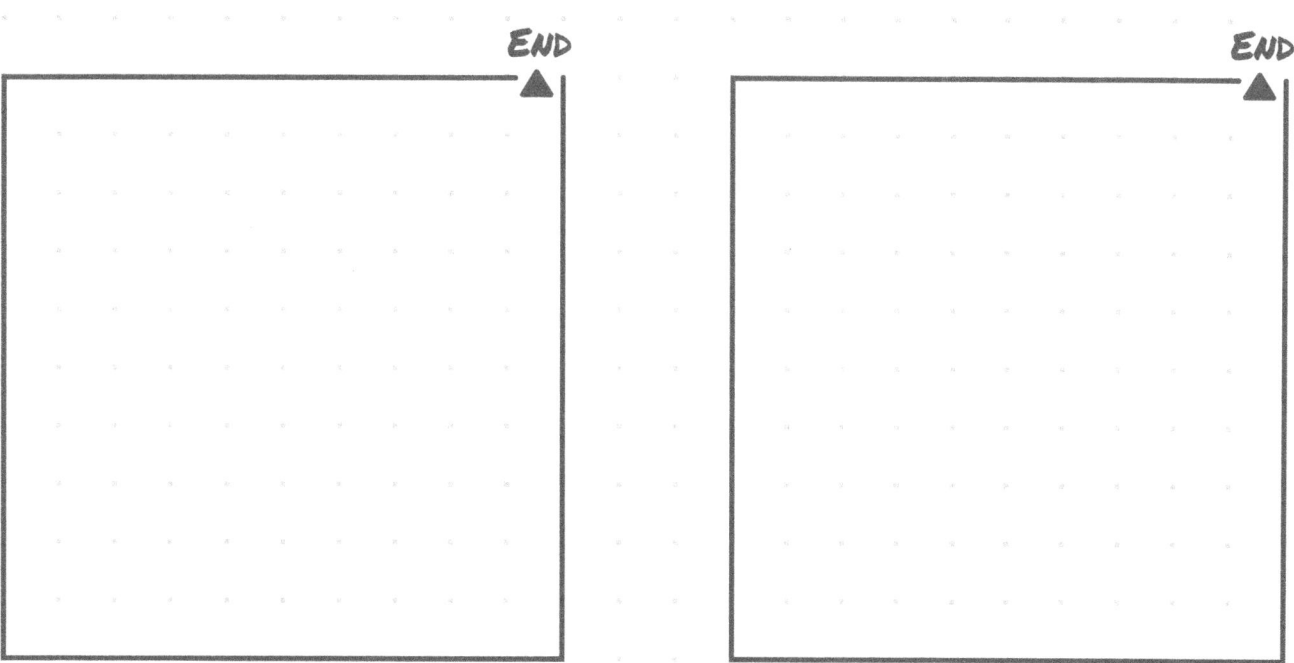

Three-Key, One-Door Mazes

Next, let's imagine that the player must collect three keys before they can exit the maze. An example maze is shown to the right.

Notice that now the dead ends feel rewarding, rather than disappointing.

Try creating your own three-key maze here. It can be planar or non-planar.

TRY IT OUT!

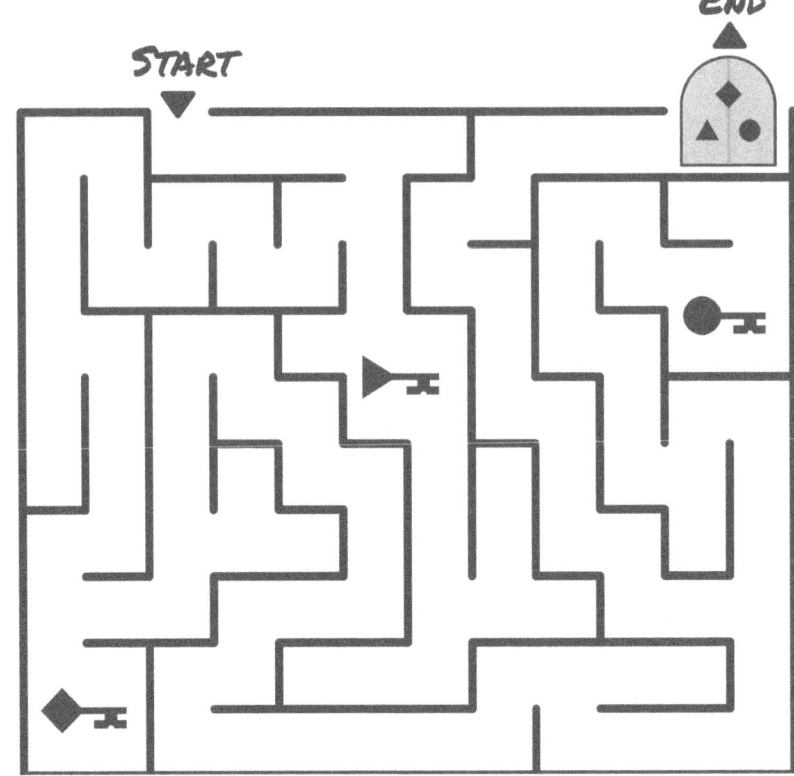

Try making a three-key, one-door maze. The ending has been placed. Choose your own starting point.

END ▲

Three-Key, Three-Door Mazes

A natural extension is to add three doors that correspond to your three keys. This not only forces the player to explore dead ends but turns the order of that exploration into a puzzle. An example maze is shown to the right.

Make a couple of your own three-key, three-door mazes.

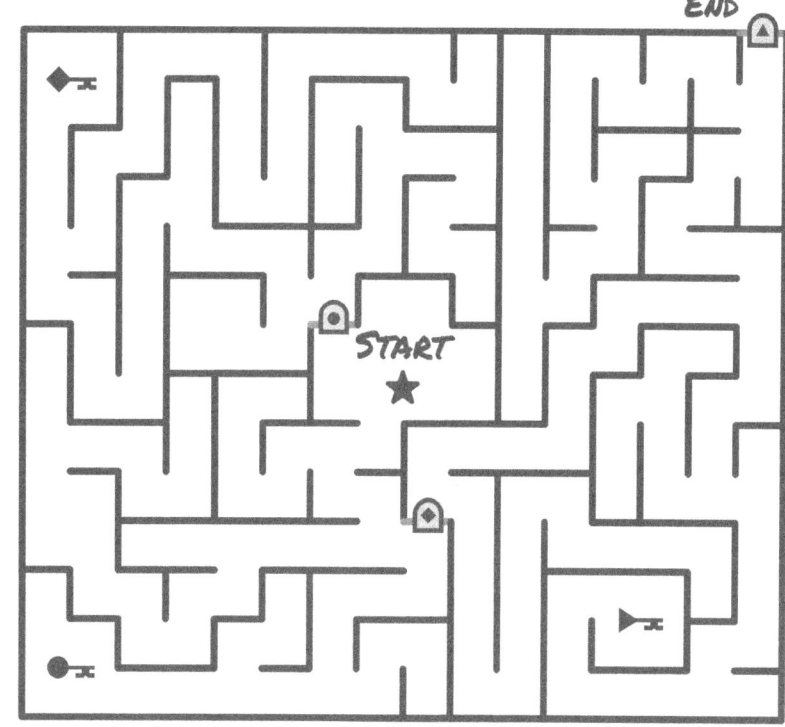

TRY IT OUT!

Try making a three-key, three-door maze here. The ending has been placed. Choose your own starting point.

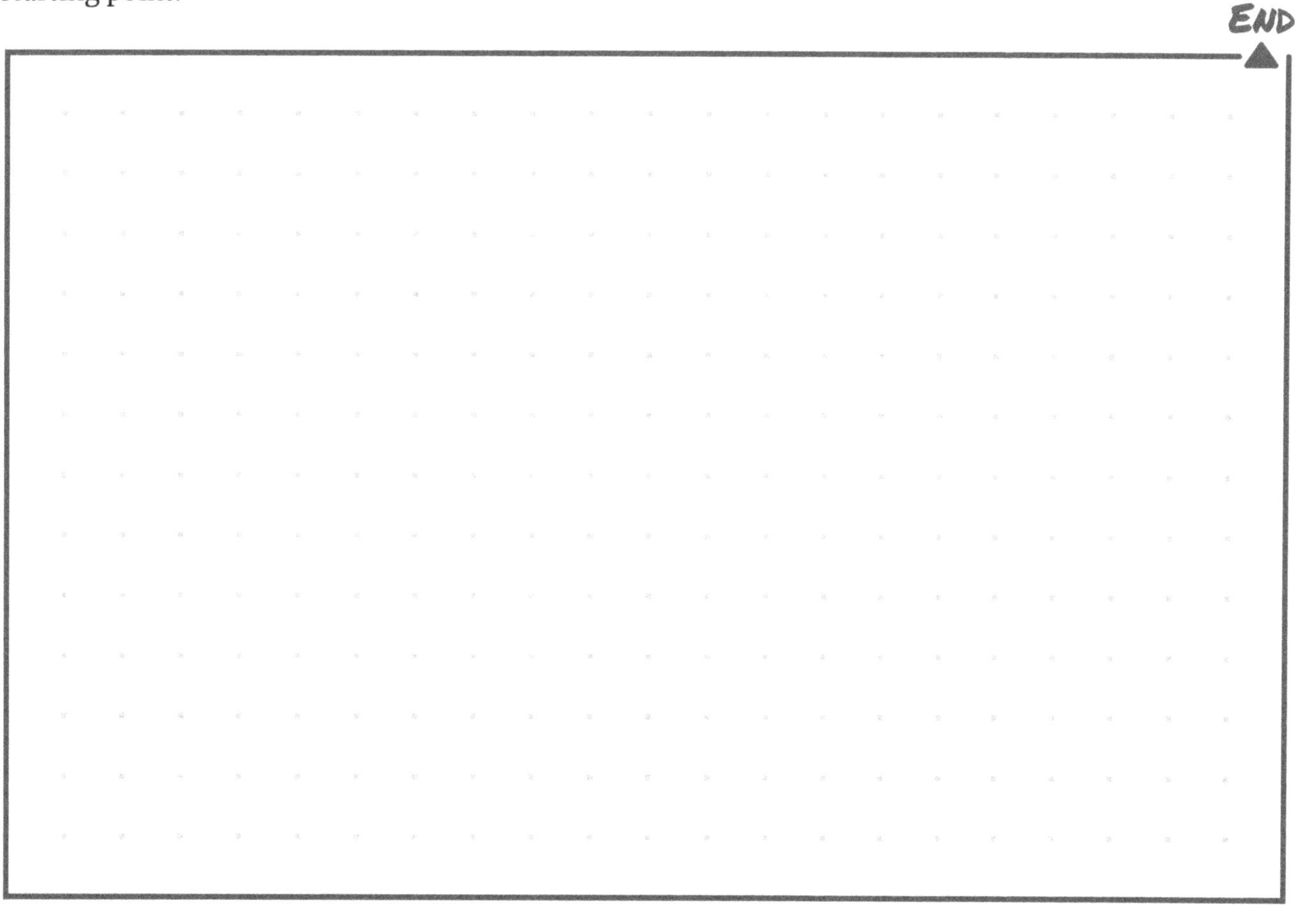

END

3D Mazes

What about a maze on a cube? To create a maze here you'll need to have a solid understanding of how six squares wrap to form one cube; you'll notice that each open side of the following diagram has a letter that matches the letter of the side that it will join. How will you visualize a 3D space in 2D? How will you think through paths that must intersect over folds of the cube? Want to vizualize this in 3D space? Head to *gamedesignersworkbook.com* and download the free papercraft version!

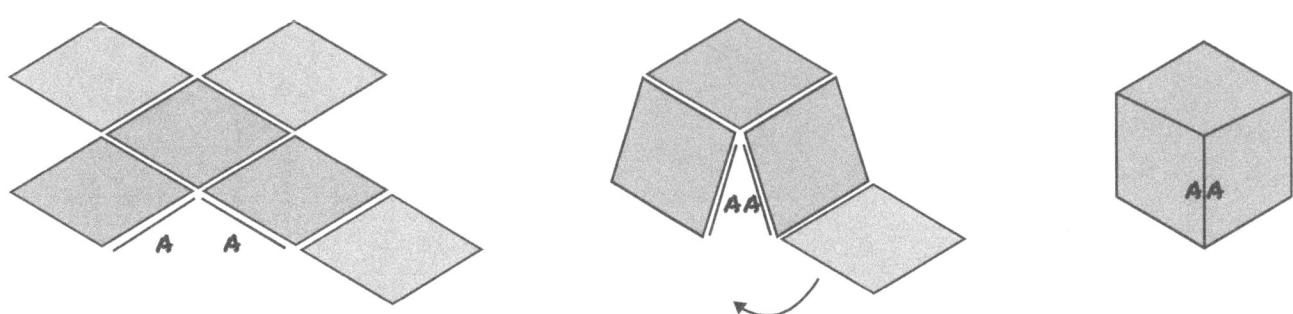

TRY IT OUT! Try making a cube maze here.

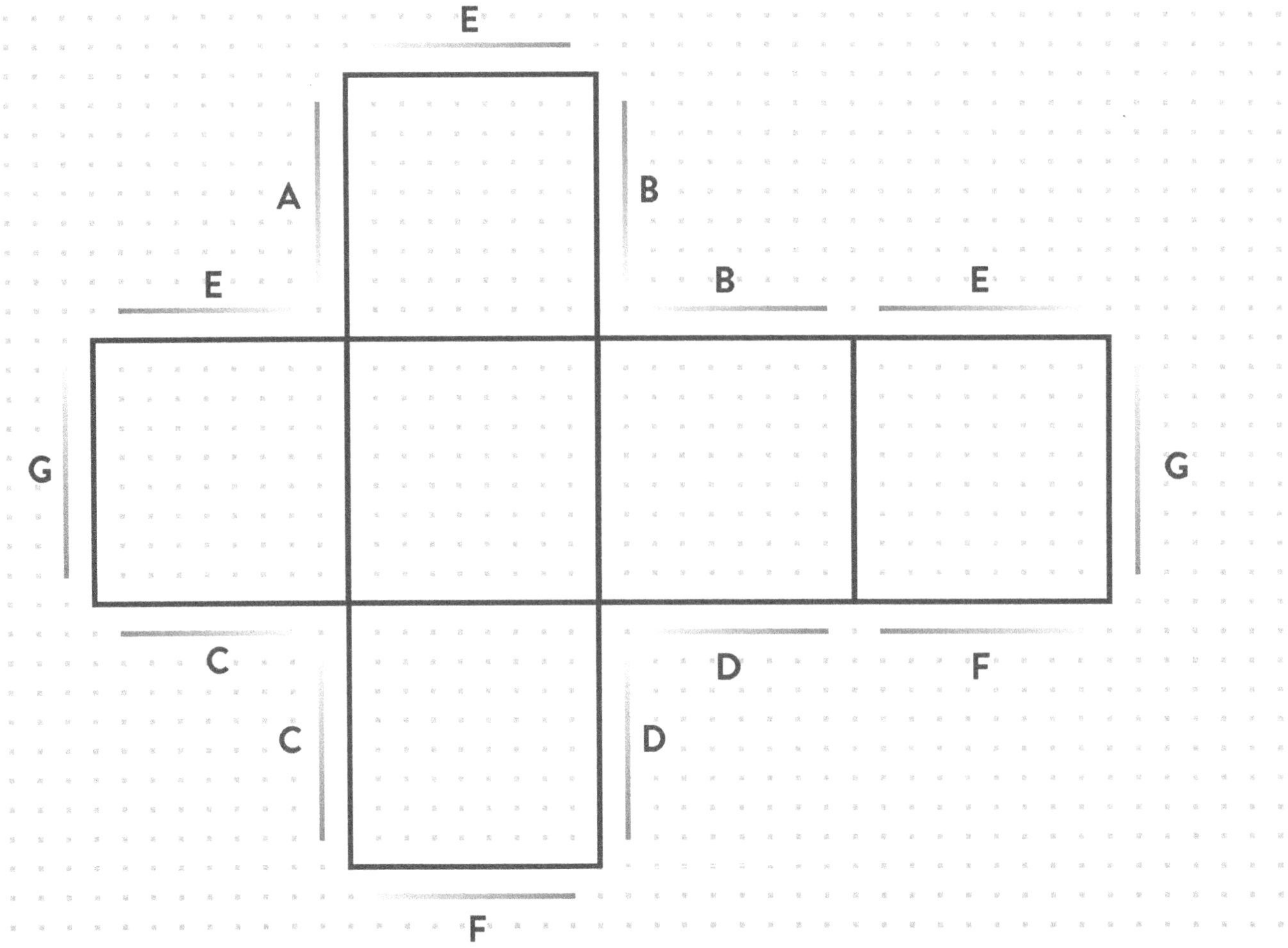

E

A   B

E   B   E

G   G

C   D   F

C   D

F

Lastly, let's look at mazes on some more exotic geometry. When a rectangle "wraps"—that is, items that exit on the left emerge on the right and items that exit on the bottom emerge on the top—we call that surface "toroidal." That's because you could wrap the rectangle around a toroid (a donut shape) and the edges would be connected in the same way.

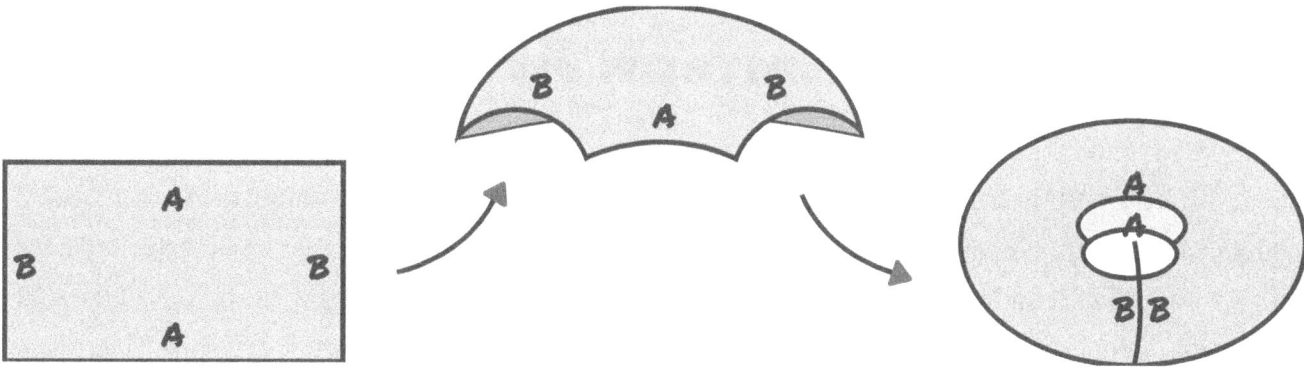

TRY IT OUT!

Try making a toroidal maze here! Use one star as your start and one as your end. Try to visualize how the rectangle wraps onto a toroid as you build your maze.

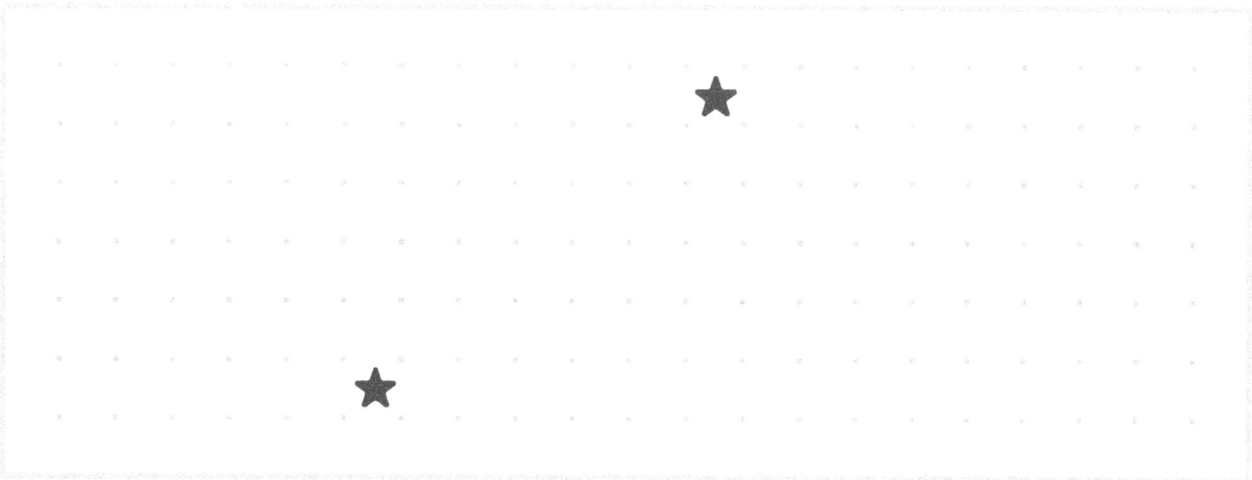

What a Concept: Accessibility

When we mention accessibility, your mind most likely goes to addressing disability, but it's really just about difference. Whether we acknowledge it or not, we all need special accommodations from the people and environment around us. Some adjustments relate to culture or to personal taste, and a few stem from medical conditions. The beauty of attempting to satisfy as many of those accommodations as possible is that they usually improve the experience for everyone.

Consider the stereotypical example of a wheelchair ramp. While it may have been built explicitly for wheelchair users, a ramp helps people with all kinds of mobility issues, mild or severe. It also lets people navigate more easily with strollers or bicycles. A ramp is handy when moving cargo in a hand-truck or cart. Naturally, folks who would normally use stairs can use the ramp, too. As game designers, we don't typically need to build literal ramps, but other accessibility features work much the same way.

The following are some of the most common accessibility considerations we deal with in both digital and tabletop game design:

Physical Space
- Can players get to where the game is?
- Can they comfortably use the interface?
- Can they see the display or output?

Impaired Vision
- Is the type large enough?
- Are we meeting minimum contrast of 3:1 and preferably 4.5:1 for elements that need to stand out?
- Can the game work with screen readers?
- Could we use voice-over instead of, or in addition to, text?

Color Vision Deficiency (Color Blindness)
- Can we use brightness, shape, and/or motion instead of color?
- When messaging through color, can we use colors that contrast even for people with color vision deficiency (e.g., orange against blue)?

Dyslexia

- Are our fonts weighted low on the characters?
- Can we allow players to switch fonts, since different people find different fonts more readable?
- Is the type, it bears repeating, as large as possible?

Motor Skills

- Are fast reflexes necessary?
- Does the player need to make smooth consistent motions, such as drag and drop?

Memory

- Is there information the player needs to retain that can't be found and referenced or determined through (consequence-free) experimentation?

Motion Sickness

- What does the game look like when the camera moves quickly?
- For VR, are the framerates high enough? Can we eliminate all accelerations of players?

Epilepsy

- Have we eliminated flashing patterns that could trigger a seizure?

Deafness

- Are instructions and story represented anywhere other than audio? Does the game have captions?

Keep in mind that there are some accommodations that either dilute the concept of a game too far or are simply logistically infeasible. Audiences are usually understanding of such limitations as long as they are stated clearly up-front (before a purchase or investment of time). It's impossible to make a game for absolutely everyone, but developers need to make tough decisions about whom to support, and need to be honest about who's excluded and why they're being left out.

A Note on Empathy

Design firm IDEO defines empathy as: "A deep understanding of the problems of the people whom you are designing for." There is a reason playtesting is so important. It shines a bright light on all the areas of your game that weren't designed with your players in mind. You can start building empathy—and understanding your players (to a point)—before the playtesting phase by putting yourself in their shoes. For instance, view your work through a colorblindness simulator: Sim Daltanism and Color Oracle are free on Mac and PC, respectively. What happens if you try to play your game with only a keyboard? Is your game still playable with the sound turned down? Can you play your game using only one hand? These questions are good, but at some point, you will want to sit down and watch someone play your game. Not only will your design get better, but you will build a game for the people you are designing for.

Thinking It Through

Let's work through a few different kinds of games to figure out how to make them more accessible.

The game is a first-person Tekken-style 3D fighting game in an arcade cabinet. Players need to wear polarized 3D glasses to view the game in 3D (without them, the game looks doubled and blurry). The game is controlled via joystick and arcade buttons. The camera controls are limited, but the player is able to sidestep quickly in either direction. The game can be played by two people side-by-side or in a single-player mode where the player fights a series of computer-controlled combatants.

How would you make this game more accessible?

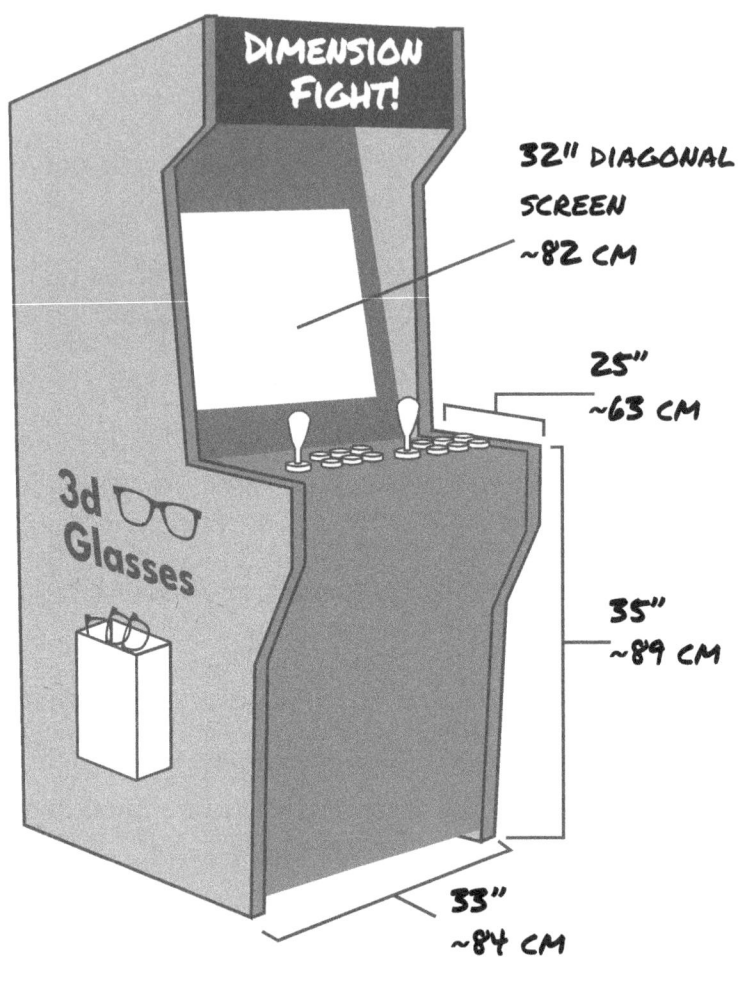

Let's take a look at this proposed user interface for a PC point-and-click adventure inventory screen. Players can drag within the inventory grid to rearrange or to combine objects. For example, combining a hammer and a harmonica might create a hammeronica (don't ask me what that means). Players can also drag an item entirely out of the grid to attempt to use it on something in the immediate environment. There is no way to discard an item you have found.

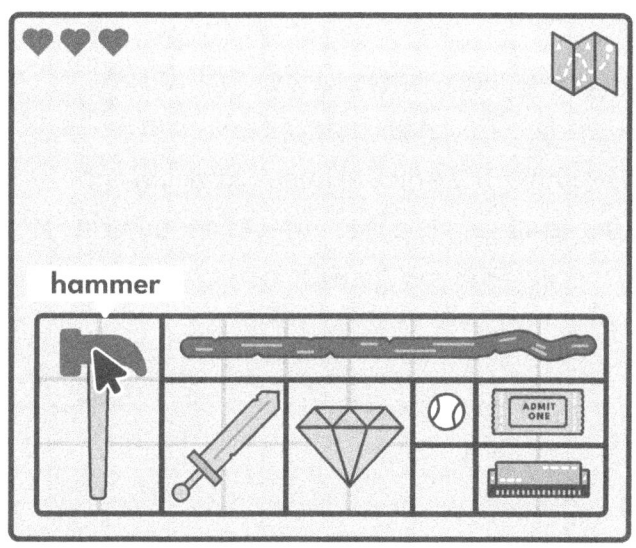 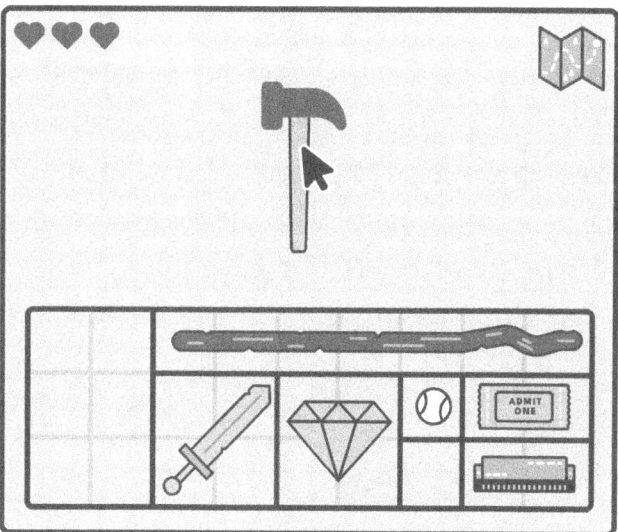

HOW WOULD YOU MAKE THIS GAME MORE ACCESSIBLE?

It's possible that those challenges felt a bit like a quiz. Giving an example of an inherently innaccessible game without giving away potential solutions can be challenging because sometimes the inaccessible portions of it are self-evident in its description. If I say, "Here is a board game with very small text and pieces that are red and green, some solutions are apparent; increase the text size, and make the pieces different shapes as well as different colors. Rather than modifying an existing game, or trying to make an inherently inaccessible game accessible, let's design a new game concept.

Go through the list of accessibility considerations on pages 18 and 19, and pick two that you don't personally struggle with. Then, conceptualize some potential game ideas that you *think* will be playable by people you are desiging this game for. For example, if we picked impaired vision and memory issues, maybe we could design a tactile stacking strategy game that always communicates its current state, or a virtual reality game that challenges the player to navigate their environment using echo location and haptics.

Think Like a Game Designer

How did it feel coming up with those ideas? If it felt easier than you thought it would, that's because often creative constraints are the best way to brainstorm new ideas, unlock an problem, or even create a theme around an existing design. In that way, they hardly feel like constraints at all.

Now that you've got some ideas, start fleshing them out. Pick one that feels the clearest to you. I'm willing to bet you'll be surprised at how fun of a game design it turns out to be.

Cross-Training: Schematic Drawing

Much of the work of game design is recording your ideas in a way that others can understand them. In industrial design and architecture, designers wrestle with much the same challenge. They have developed some techniques for specifying 3D ideas on 2D surfaces, which may be useful to your practice as well.

1. Arrange Views Like an Unfolded Box

When drawing an object, you should present multiple sides of it. They should be arranged as if they were drawn onto the sides of a box and the box was then flattened. Additional angles, such as 3/4 view, can be tucked into the corners.

You don't need to include all six of the box faces, as one or more is usually either redundant or so predictable as to be unnecessary.

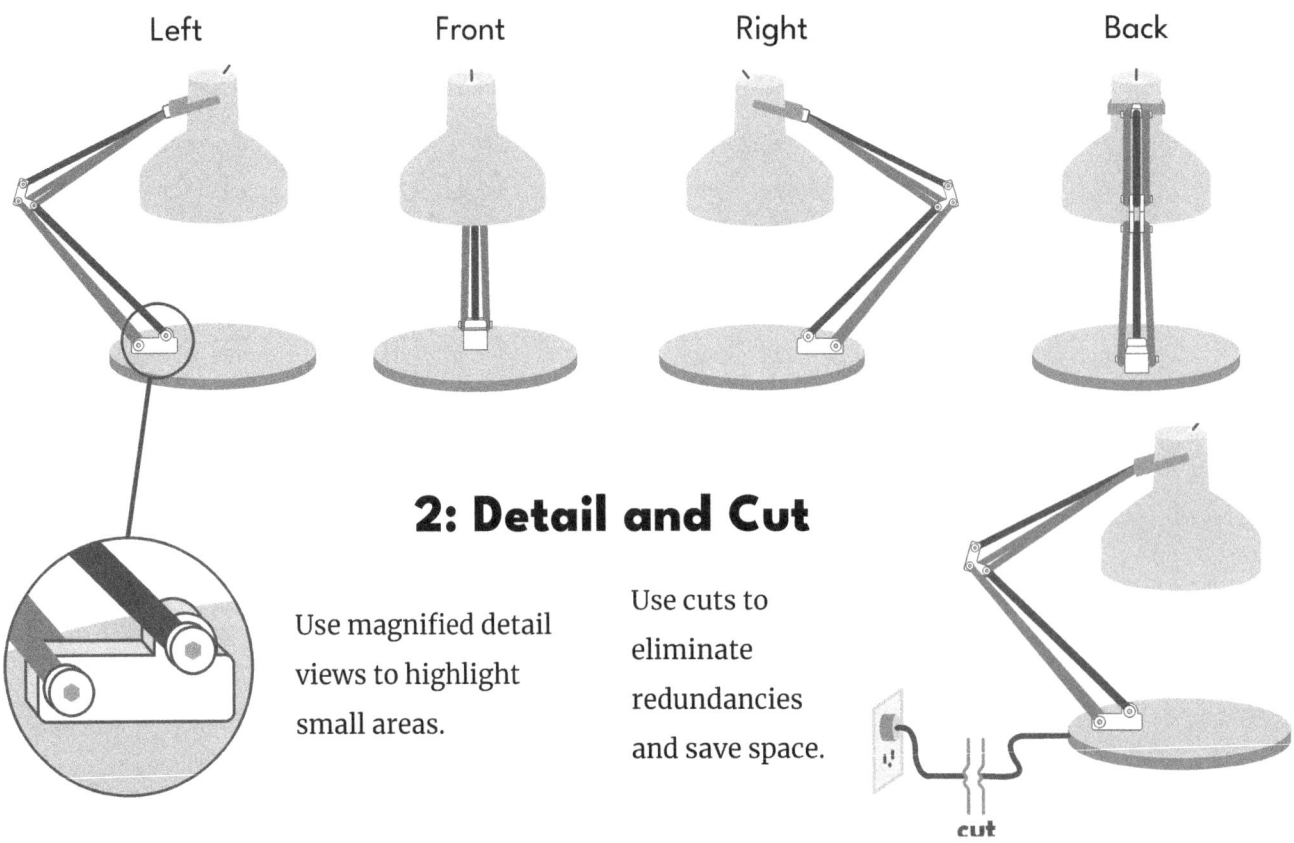

Left   Front   Right   Back

2: Detail and Cut

Use magnified detail views to highlight small areas.

Use cuts to eliminate redundancies and save space.

cut

3: Section Views

Section views can add important information about an item's inner workings.

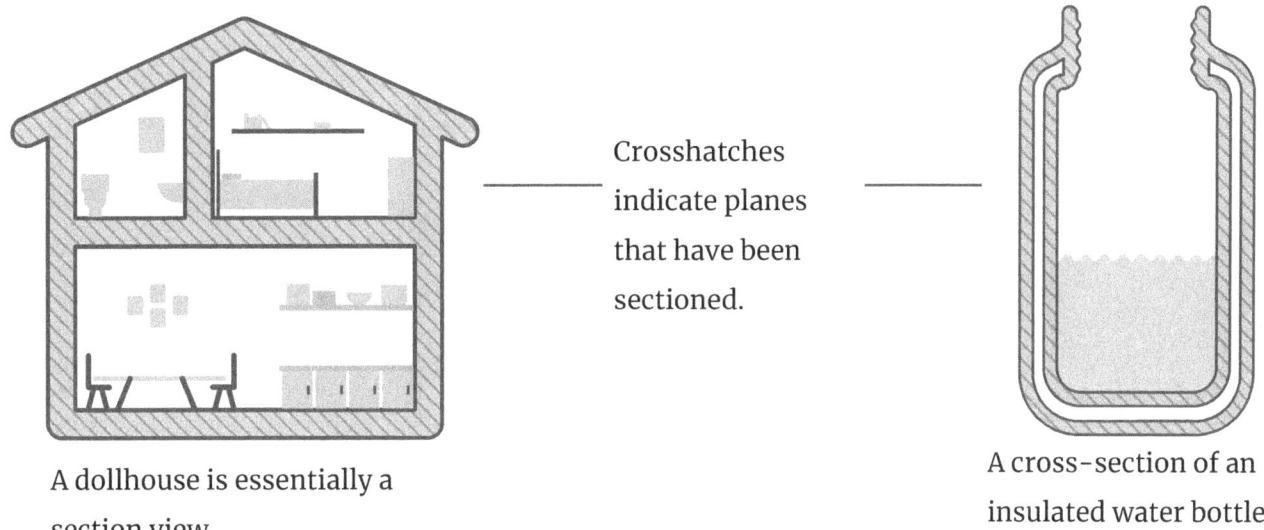

Crosshatches indicate planes that have been sectioned.

A dollhouse is essentially a section view.

A cross-section of an insulated water bottle

4: Indicate Dimensions with Extending Lines and Extent Lines

If a dimension isn't known with much precision, indicate that! The tilde (~) means "approximately."

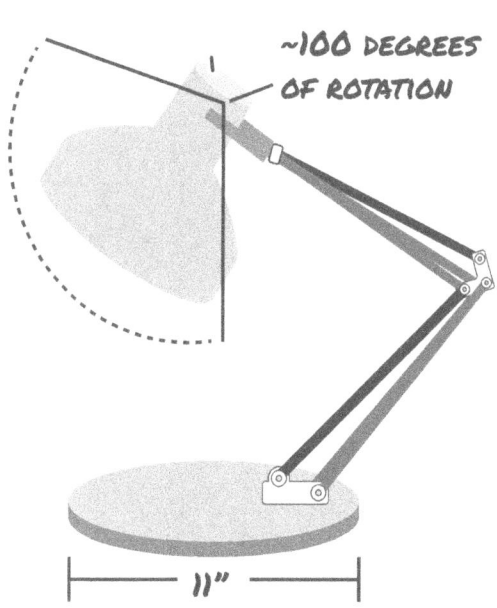

~100 DEGREES OF ROTATION

11"

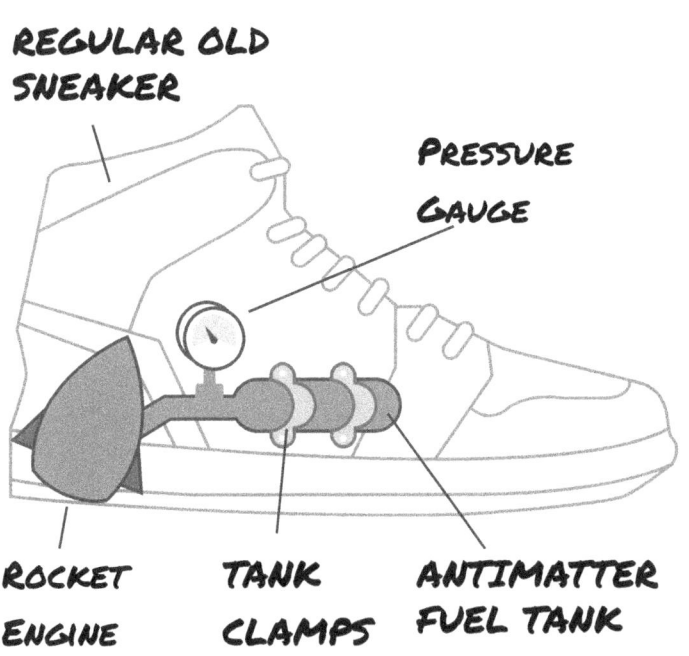

REGULAR OLD SNEAKER

PRESSURE GAUGE

ROCKET ENGINE

TANK CLAMPS

ANTIMATTER FUEL TANK

5: Label Anything and Everything

It's really not possible to have too many labels.

Your Mission, Should You Choose to Accept It (and You Should)

Choose an everyday item, perhaps something nearby. Add a fantastical element to that item, be it rockets, lasers, levitation coils, or anything you want—as long as it is utterly impractical. Draw a schematic of this new device in the following space, in as much detail as you can create.

Breaking It Down: Capturing the Feeling

Game designers often talk about their goals in terms of creating sensations and experiences for the players. This task bids you to practice translating those sorts of goals into artifacts that satisfy them.

Create a game that has a similar feeling to a solitary activity you know well. The game doesn't need to look like the activity or resemble it in any superficial way. We just want it to evoke a similar feeling.

It should be a turn-based single-player game. Here are some ideas for activities to try to capture. You can choose one of these or think of another:

- Trying to find a comfortable sleeping position when you know you don't have much time before morning
- Finding the right place to sit in a high-school cafeteria
- Pairing freshly laundered socks
- Making breakfast for your still-sleeping guests

WHAT ACTIVITY HAVE YOU CHOSEN TO CAPTURE?

HOW DOES DOING YOUR ACTIVITY MAKE YOU FEEL?

Are there any existing game mechanics that evoke a similar feeling in you?

_____

_____

_____

_____

What type of game will best capture this feeling (circle one)?

- Card Game
- Pen-and-Paper Game
- Dexterity Game
- Dice Game

- Board Game
- Digital Game
- Other

Use this space to outline a solitaire game that captures the feeling of the activity you chose:

Randomized Game Idea:
Pencil-and-Paper Games

Read on for instructions on how to use the following grid.

	A Field	**B** Goal	**C** Players	**D** Turns
•	Start with a square grid of dots.	Capture the most territory	Solo game	Taken strictly round-robin
• •	Before play, players draw squiggles that are connected on both ends to previous squiggles, thus forming a map.	Connect a row of symbols	Two-player competitive	Players continue until their turn ends
• ••	Draw a particular number of vertical lines. Next, take turns drawing short horizontal lines connecting the vertical lines.	Create a connected path from one end to the other	Three-player competitive	Players choose to take one, two, or three turns in a row
• • • •	Start with a random arrangement of dots.	Avoid taking the last turn	Two-player cooperative	Taken strictly round-robin
• • ••	Start on a preexisting page of text, like a newspaper.	Force your opponent to arrange their marks a certain way	Three-player cooperative	Players continue until their turn ends
•• ••	Start on a hexagonal grid.	Score the most points	Two-player cooperative that changes phases to competitive at some point	Players choose to take one, two, or three turns in a row

How to use random dice columns

1. Pick a number in your mind between 1 and 10.
2. Go from the top of the dice list and cross off that many dice.
3. Start using dice from there, and go down the list in sequential order.

3

✗ SKIP

✗ SKIP

✗ SKIP

- - - - - - - - - - - - - -

◀ START HERE!

USE NEXT

USE NEXT

Making Your Randomized Game

Use the dice in the margins to randomly select one box from each column in the grid. Combine the ideas from each chosen box into a game, and use the following pages to specify that game in as much detail as you can.

This randomized grid is focused on pencil-and-paper games, like tic-tac-toe, which are very important examples in this book for obvious reasons.

WRITE DOWN YOUR NEW GAME RULES:

USE THIS SPACE TO SPECIFY ANY ADDITIONAL RULES:

USE THIS SPACE TO TRY A HEX GRID-BASED GAME:

USE THIS SPACE TO TRY A SQUARE GRID-BASED GAME:

USE THIS SPACE FOR LINE OR SQUIGGLE-BASED GAMES:

Round Two! Use this space to specify any additional rules:

Use this space to try a hex grid-based game:

USE THIS SPACE TO TRY A SQUARE GRID-BASED GAME:

USE THIS SPACE FOR LINE OR SQUIGGLE-BASED GAMES:

Chapter Two

Abstract Strategy

Each move you make in the game is a way
for you to express yourself...Every reckless
agression and coy bluff, every greedy power
grab and defensive stall for time is a word, a
phrase, a statement in the language of
the game.

—Geoffrey Engelstein
& Isaac Shalev

*Building Blocks of
Tabletop Game Design*

Reflection: A Gameplay Memory

Write about an early memory you have of playing a game. What was the game? What was the context? What happened? How did it make you feel? What do you think made this incident so memorable?

A Note on Memory

A memory is not the same as an experience. Memory—especially long-term memory— is filtered through natural biases and neuronal encodings. That said, sometimes the way you remember something, distorted as it is, can be better than the original. This is the source of many of the games industry's best "spiritual successor" games. What can you learn from how your memory has reshaped the game you're reflecting on?

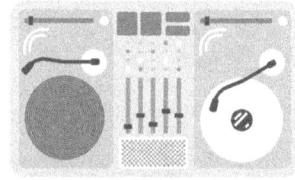

Remix: Connect Four

Connect Four is typically played vertically, dropping physical tokens into a frame between the two players. However, since players only add tokens—they never move or remove them—it can also be played as a pencil-and-paper game.

The Rules of Connect Four:

1. Connect Four takes place on a square grid seven spaces wide and seven spaces tall.

2 Two players alternate turns.

3 On a player's turn, they choose a column of the grid. They then draw a distinguishing mark (or drop a distinguishing token) in the lowest unoccupied space in that column. If a column has no unoccupied spaces, it cannot be chosen.

4 The first player to form a line of four or more of their own marks or tokens wins. The lines may be horizontal, vertical, or diagonal.

5 If the whole grid is filled and neither player has won, the game is a draw.

Here's some space to try it before you make any changes. It's okay to play against yourself, as long as you don't pick favorites. Use Xs and Os for your marks, or any other two symbols you can easily tell apart.

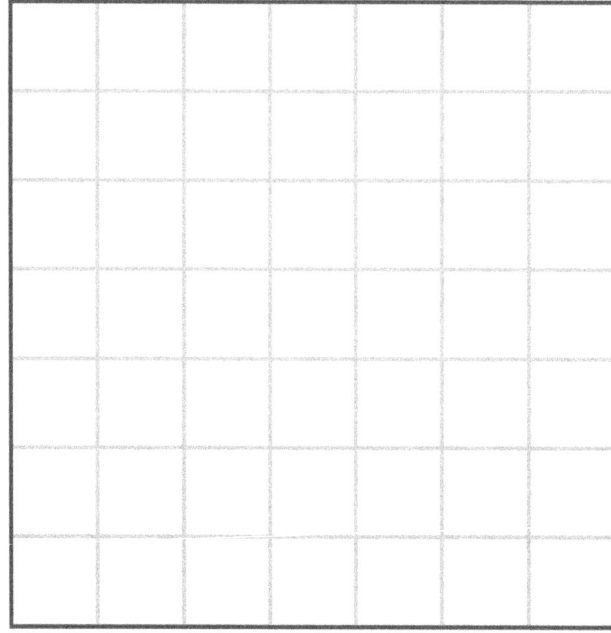

Now choose a rule to change **other than rule #1**. Think about how this change might make the game better.

REPLACEMENT FOR RULE #__

Chances are, your rule didn't work out perfectly. Make an amendment to your rule and test again.

AMENDMENT TO NEW RULE:

Finally, let the gloves come off. Make as many changes to the rules as you want, but try not to lose the spirit of Connect Four.

NEW RULES:

What a Concept: Forks

In games, a fork is when a player moves in such a way that they will have two good options for their next move and their opponent can use their intervening move to prevent only one.

Forks can be found in many games:

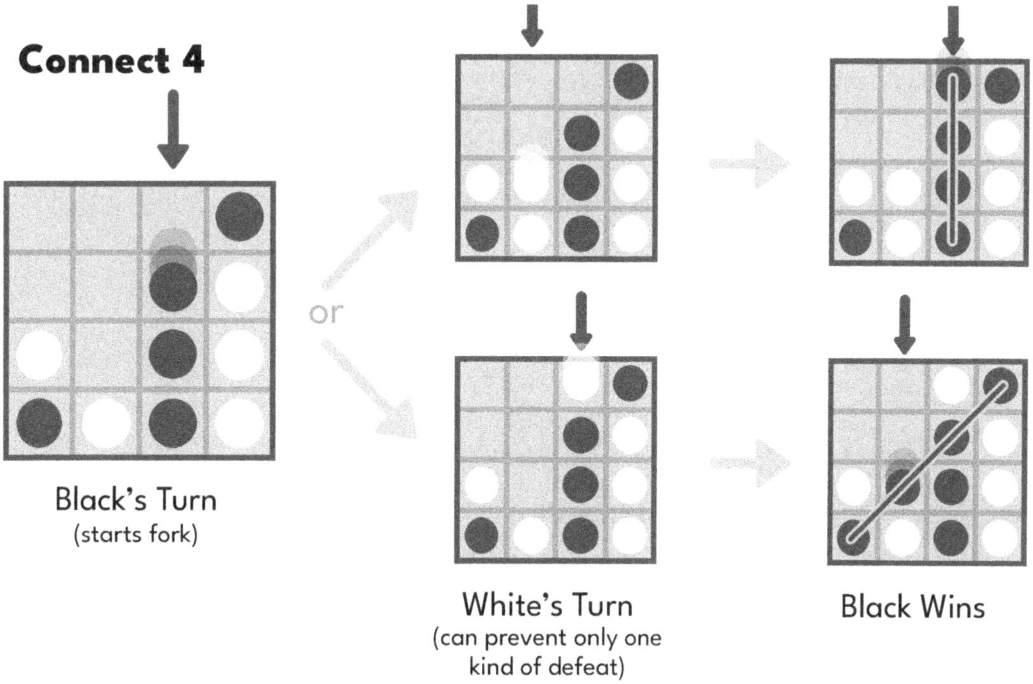

Connect 4

Black's Turn
(starts fork)

or

White's Turn
(can prevent only one
kind of defeat)

Black Wins

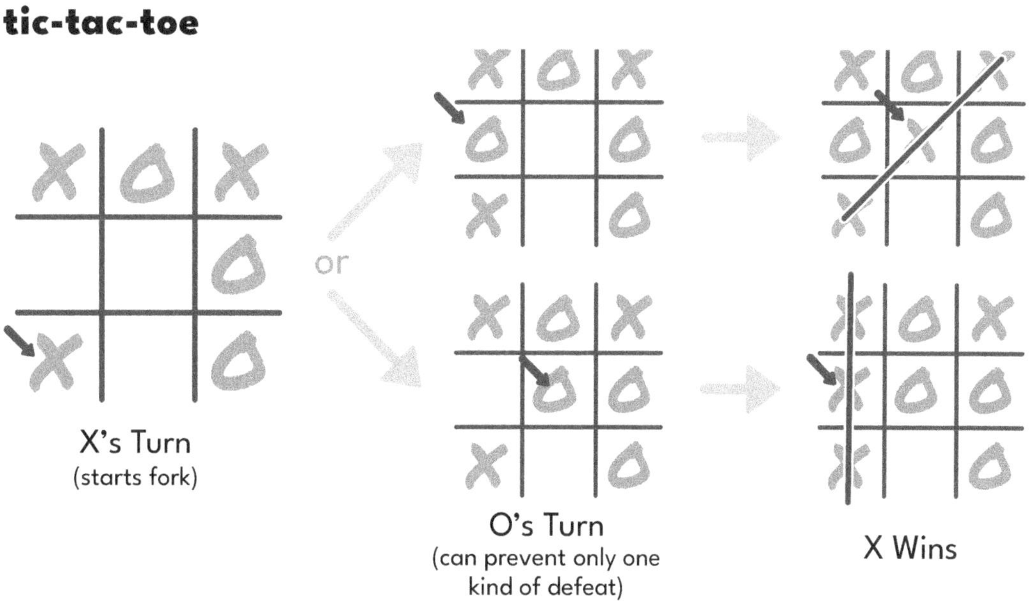

tic-tac-toe

X's Turn
(starts fork)

or

O's Turn
(can prevent only one
kind of defeat)

X Wins

Chess

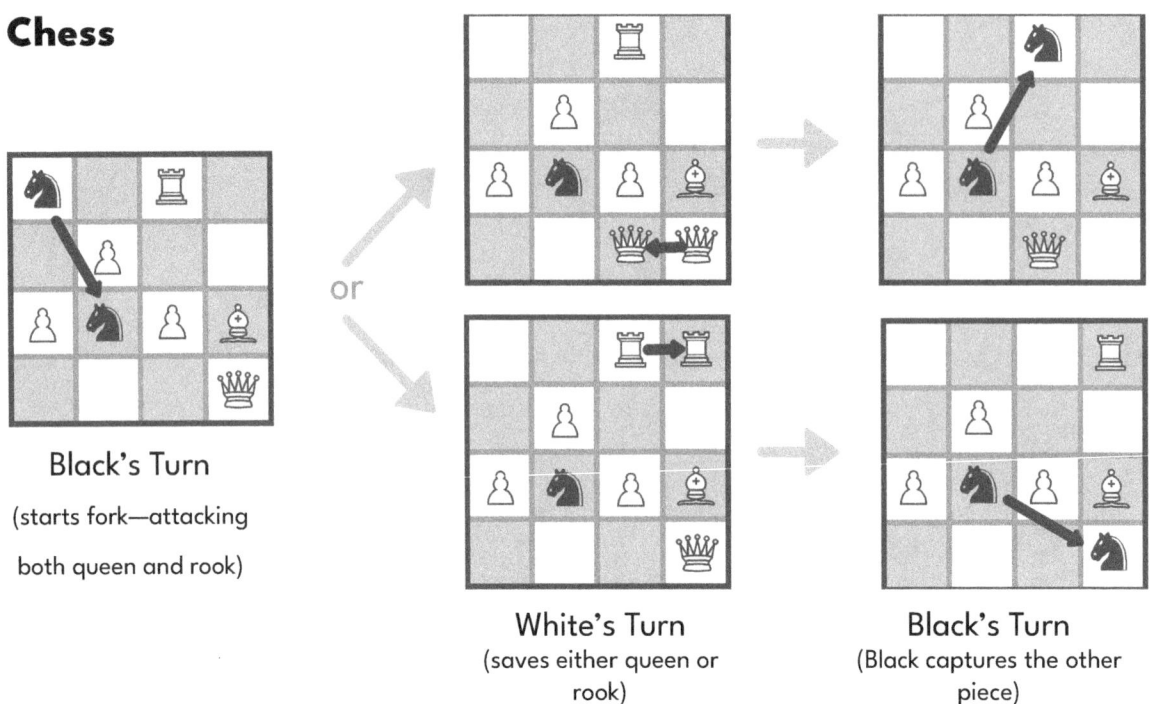

Black's Turn

(starts fork—attacking both queen and rook)

White's Turn
(saves either queen or rook)

Black's Turn
(Black captures the other piece)

Forks also occur, more subtly, in real-time games like football and fencing.

YOUR TURN

Your task is to design a simple grid-based, turn-based game for two players that allows players to employ forks. If possible, playtest your game with a friend, with the goal that they are able to create a fork without your help. Use the space below to scaffold your rules and brainstorm, and the grids on the next page to flesh out your idea. Start simple, and think checkers, not chess.

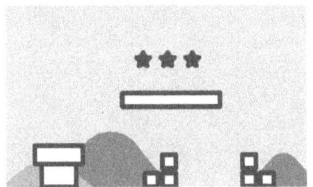

Level Design: Dots and Boxes

In this level design exercise, you'll start with a variation on the pen-and-paper game Dots and Boxes. If you're not familiar with the game, the rules are:

1. The game takes place within a rectangular grid of dots, usually 5x5 dots at minimum. This makes 4x4 spaces within the dots.

2. Two players take turns drawing lines between adjacent dots. Adjacent means horizontally or vertically, *not* diagonally.

3. If a line completes a square (or "box"), the player who drew it puts a mark within the box to indicate ownership.

4. That player must then take another turn connecting two dots with a line.

5. The game ends when all boxes in the grid have been filled. The player with the most boxes owned, wins.

Try it a few times against yourself. Use straight (·—·) and wavy (·~·) lines to help keep track of which "player" you're playing as. Notice that long chain reactions emerge.

Player —	Player ~~

Player —	Player ~~

Player —	Player ~~

You will be designing levels for a variant of this game. In this variant, the rules are the same as in the original. The differences are:

1. The grid of dots can take different (but still rectilinear) shapes.
2. The point value of each box is given by a number written inside it.
3. The winner is the player with the most points at the end of the game.

Play against yourself on the example playfields here, once again using straight and wavy lines to help remember which lines belong to which virtual player. Tally up the points in the area below each playfield.

Player —	Player ∿

Player —	Player ∿

As you could see, you have a lot of freedom in terms of the point values, as well as the geometry of the overall grid.

GIVE IT A SHOT! TRY MAKING A LARGER PLAYFIELD HERE:

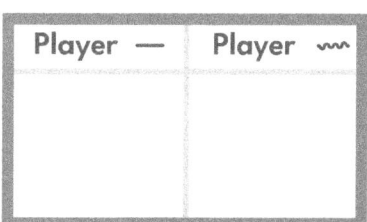

Player —	Player ∿

Think Like a Game Designer

Test the playfield you created. Was it satisfying to play on? Think a bit about what makes for an interesting play-space for this variant, and then have another try or two here.

Player —	Player ∿

Player —	Player ∿

Player —	Player ∿

What Is...MDA?

MDA stands for "mechanics, dynamics, aesthetics." It's a framework for game design introduced in 2004 by Hunicke, LeBlanc, and Zubek, and has been expanded upon elsewhere. The basic idea is that since the essential activity of a game is to play (rather than viewing, reading, listening, etc.), the part of your game that needs to be worked out first are the "play" parts. A game idea may start with any part of the game experience, including the mood, the look, the story, or the sound. However, what makes a game a game are the mechanics. What can the player do? How does the game world react to the player's actions?

Once the mechanics are tentatively established, the framework suggests that your next duty is to tackle the game's dynamics. These are the ways game elements interrelate to create more complex systems. In other words, what makes it harder for a player to predict the consequences of their actions?

Again, once the mechanics have been provisionally set, the designer can begin to tackle the aesthetics of the game. That includes our colloquial understanding of aesthetics, like how the elements look and sound, their stories, the setting, and the themes of the game. It also means the broad types of play and the emotional effects you expect the game to have on the player. Aesthetics should ideally tie themselves in some way to the mechanics, making them easier to learn and to intuit. So, for example, if the mechanics of the game involve stacking cubes, perhaps your protagonist should be a warehouse manager. Perhaps it should feel challenging, or maybe more casual.

Each of these steps is meant to be iterative within themselves and also to trigger a reevaluation of the steps before. A system's dynamics may suggest new mechanics. An aesthetic choice may map itself to the mechanics and dynamics in such a way as to force new constraints upon, or open new possibilities for, both.

Fascinatingly, the player encounters these components in the opposite order, first experiencing the game's aesthetics, then confronting its dynamics, and finally understanding the game well enough to parse its mechanics.

Your task is to briefly identify the mechanics, dynamics, and aesthetics of three games you're familiar with. Here's an example:

Game: Pac-Man

- Mechanics: Move around a toroidal maze in cardinal directions. Touch dots to get points. Avoid enemies to subtract a life. Clear all dots to move to the next level.
- Dynamics: Enemies are distinct and have unique player-seeking behavior. Special dots reverse the predator/prey relationship.
- Aesthetics: Setting is abstract. Enemies are ghosts. Protagonist is a circular mouth with eyes.

Game:

Mechanics:

Dynamics:

Aesthetics:

Game:

Mechanics:

Dynamics:

Aesthetics:

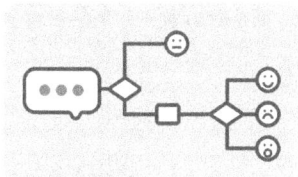

Narrative Design: Abstract Strategy

Choose an abstract strategy game that you know well, such as chess, Go, backgammon, draughts, etc. This exercise is about retrofitting the abstract strategy game of your choice to generate a story as it is played.

The Setting

First, think of a setting—a place and time. Choose something congruous for the game board of your chosen game and possible placements of the pieces, which will represent the characters in your story. Is the playfield the suburban neighborhood all the pieces live in? Is each space a condo in a residential skyscraper? Are the spaces lockers in a middle school hallway? Is it a continuous space, like an Olympic-sized public pool, that is just broken up into discrete spaces for the sake of the game?

WHEN AND WHERE DOES THE GAME TAKE PLACE?

Your Cast of Characters

Next you'll need to assign characters to all the pieces, or, if more appropriate, create a bank of characters that can be assigned to the pieces as they come into play. Every character should at the least have a name, a defining characteristic, and a desire. If the character is non-human, you should also know what sort of being they are.

The Moveset

The last piece of this narrative framework is to understand what each of the interactions in the game could mean, narratively. For instance, if you chose a game of checkers set in an office full of cutthroat businesspeople, perhaps capturing a piece means forcing them out of the company and increasing your own influence in the corporate hierarchy.

What is each piece's moveset? For example, in chess, your pieces can move, take enemy pieces, threaten your opponent's king (check), and achieve victory (checkmate). What do each of these actions mean, narratively?

LIST YOUR CHARACTERS & THEIR MOVESET HERE:

Name:

Characteristic(s):	Moveset:
Desire:	

Name:

Characteristic(s):	Moveset:
Desire:	

Name:

Characteristic(s):	Moveset:
Desire:	

Name:

Characteristic(s):	Moveset:
Desire:	

The Story

Now that you have your characters and possible moves listed, let's craft a story. Play a game against yourself and list the moves in the left column (or find the moves from someone else's game). On the right, assign narrative meaning to the moves and write out their story.

MOVES   STORY

Was your framework detailed enough to easily generate a satisfying story from a series of moves? If not, reflect on what you might alter or add to the system.

Breaking It Down: Discretizing Time and Space

Think of an activity that's normally done in a continuous fashion, like doing the Macarena, knitting a scarf, or splitting firewood. Try to choose something that doesn't involve much decision-making.

First, try to break down the activity into steps. How could you convert your continuous activity into a turn-based one?

Next, how would you best represent the space of the action in a grid or a graph?

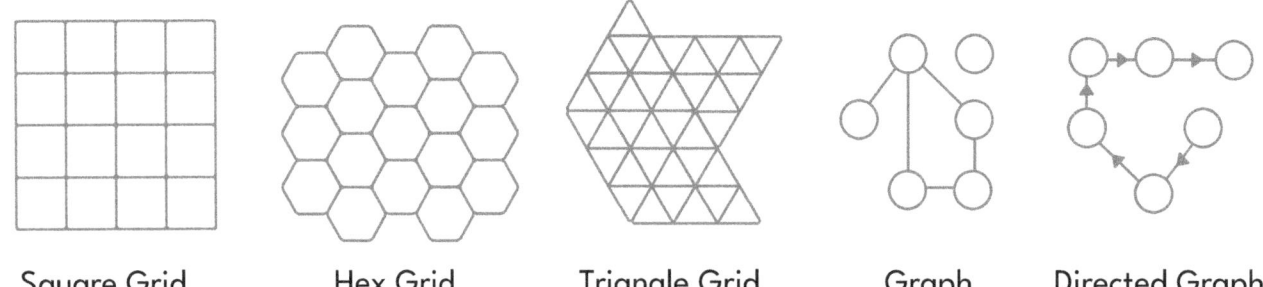

| Square Grid | Hex Grid | Triangle Grid | Graph | Directed Graph |

What would the cells or nodes of your grid or graph represent? What are the conditions that cause an element of this action to move from one cell or node to another? If there's an unpredictable component of the action, how can it be represented with the random dice column? Please make a full description in the space provided. For example, if I wanted to discretize cooking in a kitchen, I could use the graph to show moving between the locations of the fridge, sink, and stove.

GIVE IT A SHOT! DESCRIBE YOUR DISCRETIZED ACTION:

Embedding

Notice that some grids and graphs can
be made to emulate one another.

Need to think visually? Use the space here and on the following page:

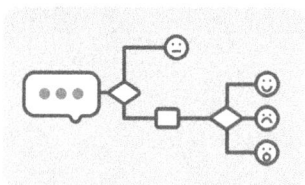

Narrative Design: Theming

A game idea can begin in lots of ways. Perhaps the game is inspired by something from the creator's life or something from the news. Maybe it's influenced by another work of art—a book, a song, or even another game. If you love narrative, it's possible that the first thing you think of will be the game's story. However, since games are a procedural art form, it's more likely that a game idea will begin with what the player does and how the game responds. Narrative usually comes after. This process of imposing a narrative, and especially the setting, is called "theming."

Themes come in two varieties: manifestation and dramatic. A manifestation theme is the part that you see right away. Where are you? Is this a world you recognize? Is this a medieval fantasy with elves and wizards? Is it a space opera, where interstellar travel is easy and alien species are plentiful? Choosing a manifestation theme gives the player a better idea of what they can expect to see. You can use those expectations to help your players learn the game, or you can subvert those expectations to capitalize on the players' surprise.

Dramatic theme is the underlying message of the game. Dramatic themes can usually be summed up as short statements of belief about the way the world works, or how it ought to. Examples of dramatic themes include "love conquers all," "blood is thicker than water," and "you can't cheat an honest man." The truth of these statements is irrelevant. What's important is that they convey a point of view.

Theming can also be heavy or light. A game like Monopoly is heavily themed, in that all the mechanics, images, and text support the idea that the player is a budding real estate tycoon. On the other end of the spectrum is chess, which is themed as a medieval battle but doesn't incorporate many elements to support that theme, other than the names and shapes of the pieces. Of course there are many abstract games, like Tetris, which remain entirely unthemed.

Imagine that you are a narrative designer who has been hired to develop a theme for a new digital adaptation of an abstract tabletop game. They're not sure how much they'd like to commit to the theme, so you'll need to pitch two versions of your concept, one lightly themed and the other more heavily themed.

First, choose and circle an abstract game to theme for this digital adaptation.

- Go
- Connect Four
- Mancala
- Chinese Checkers
- Backgammon
- Dominoes
- Stratego
- Hearts
- Yahtzee
- Uno
- Parcheesi
- Tag

Next, try to think of a dramatic theme. What do you think is the point of view this game has within it? What does the game say about being human?

What would be the manifestation theme? Describe how you would turn this into a **heavily themed** experience. What kind of world is it? Who or what do the players represent? What do their actions imply for this world?

Next, we need a more lightly themed version of the same game. You can choose to either tone down the heavily themed concept you just described or create a new concept that doesn't place as much emphasis on the setting and narrative.

Randomized Game Idea: Abstract Strategy

Read on for instructions on how to use the following grid.

	A Piece Movement	**B** Piece Abilities	**C** Number of Pieces	**D** Grid Size
•	All pieces move the same way.	Capture opponents' pieces by jumping over them with your own.	Each player starts with 16 pieces.	6x6 grid
••	Pieces do not move at all, but change state.	Capture opponents' pieces by moving into their space with your own.	Each player starts with 14 pieces.	6x7 grid
•••	Each player has two types of pieces which move differently.	Capture opponents' pieces by trapping them between your own.	Each player starts with 12 pieces.	7x7 grid
::	Each player has one piece that is more powerful than all the rest.	Add a piece to the board every turn.	Each player starts with 8 pieces.	7x8 grid
:•:	Most pieces move simply, but a few have special abilities.	Add a piece to the board when there's a certain arrangement of pieces.	Each player starts with 6 pieces.	6x8 grid
:::	Every piece moves differently.	Pieces never leave or enter the board during the game.	Each player starts with 4 pieces.	8x8 grid

Use the dice in the margins to randomly select one box from each column in the grid. Combine the ideas from each chosen box into a game, and use the following pages to specify that game in as much detail as you can.

YOUR TURN

Write down your new game design here, including any additional rules. You'll lay out your game on the following pages.

Additional Notes:

Additional Notes:

Chapter Three

Story

Every character should want something, even if it is only a glass of water.

—Kurt Vonnegut

Cross-Training: Storyboarding

In film and TV production, storyboarding is used to communicate the vision of a director or animator to the rest of their team. It is a way of visualizing a series of key moments from a continuous motion picture to capture how they want the audience to experience them.

As a game designer, you'll need to express a desired sequence of moments in a visual way, too. Sometimes, as in planning videogame cutscenes, you're representing a linear activity in a linear way. Other times you'll want to convey an example user story, a single user's experience, within a nonlinear system. In either case, storyboarding is an essential tool in the communication process between a game designer and the rest of their team.

Storyboards read similar to comic books, where each panel could represent a several-minutes-long shot or a fraction of a second, and their interpretation must be inferred from context and from the description. Here's an example:

```
EXT. DESERT - DAY
TIM dangles over the ravine, held
by TOM. "Please," says TIM.
```

```
Suddenly TOM's face drops and his
muscles slacken.  TIM has fallen.
TOM whispers "I'm sorry."
```

Take notice of a few things about the example panels:

1. The drawings are not high in detail. They convey only what's necessary.
2. The descriptions don't mention the mental state of the character, or really anything that won't be seen or heard by the audience.

These are both true because storyboarding is an inherently intermediate art form. It is a bridge between the screenplay and the film. To make the storyboards overly detailed would needlessly constrain the costume designers, production designers, makeup artists, etc. To describe the mental state of the character would be limiting to the actors.

Storyboards can also depict camera moves and lens changes.

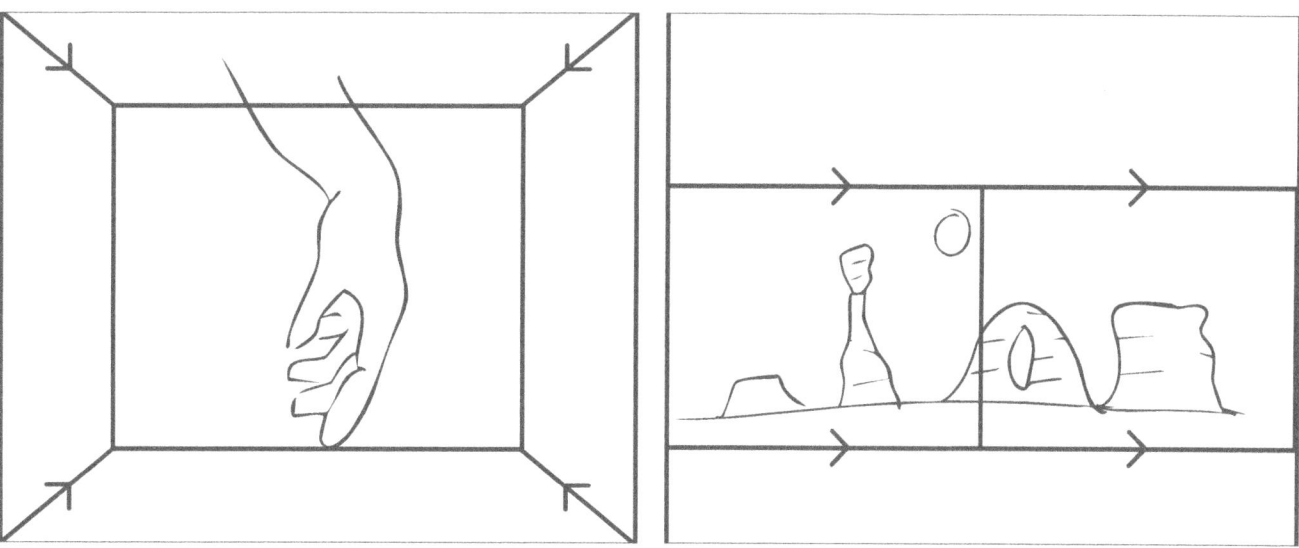

We ZOOM IN to a close-up on TOM's limp hand.

We PAN RIGHT across the surreal desert landscape.

In each case, the starting frame is connected to the ending frame by lines that join the corners and that have arrows to indicate the direction of travel.

Referencing a Camera Move

Here is a cheat-sheet of camera and lens moves. Camera moves use a common set of terms. This allows other people to better envision your idea in their mind as they look through your storyboards.

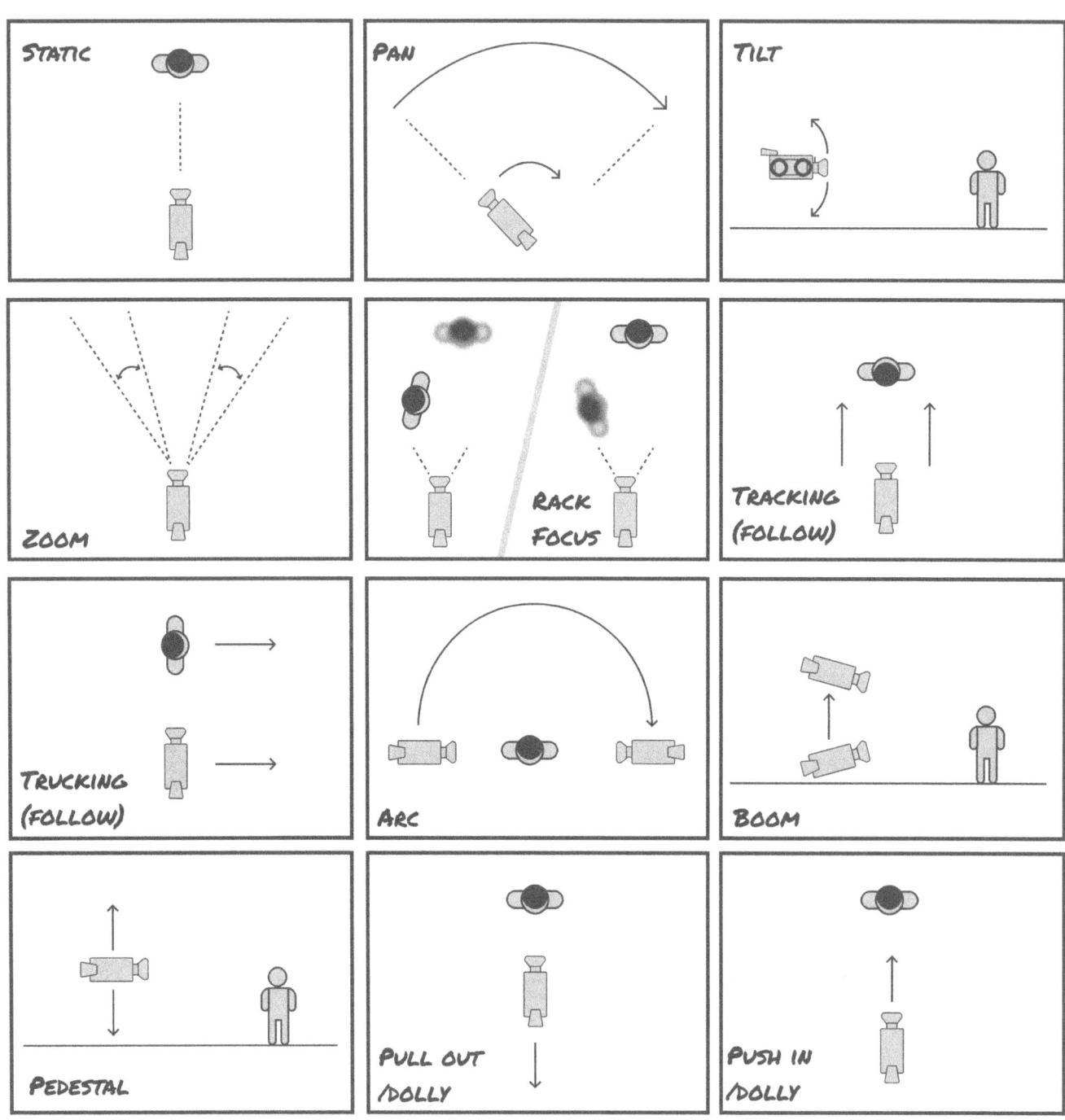

- **Static shots** are focused on clarity. They show emotion and action with purity. A whole film can be made up of static shots, and they are the most common type for good reason.
- **Pans** and **tilts** are often used for point of view.
- **Tracking** and **trucking** are used to follow the flow of a linear action, like walking.
- **Arc shots** are often meant to convey awe.
- A **pedestal** is used to establish a new thing literally from head to toe.
- A **boom** indicates a change in hierarchy, where the subject seems to become larger or smaller.
- A **rack focus** is literally and metaphorically a change in focus.
- **Dollying** in or out can be used to show a part of a whole or to show the whole attached to a part. In either case it is essentially used for context and exposition.
- A **zoom** is similar to dollying, but has the side-effect of flattening or deepening the background around the subject.
- A **push/pull** might tell the audience that something has just changed between the character and their environment.

If you've watched any movies or TV, you've seen each type of shot hundreds of times. You just saw some examples of why you might use a certain shot, but there are lots more reasons not covered, and not yet imagined.

There are also some well-known combinations of camera moves that have their own names. A boom up/down is a combination of a pedestal and a tilt. An arc is a special kind of truck-and-pan combination that rotates the camera around the subject. A push/pull is the famous dolly/zoom combination used in *Jaws*, *Vertigo*, *Goodfellas*, and many more.

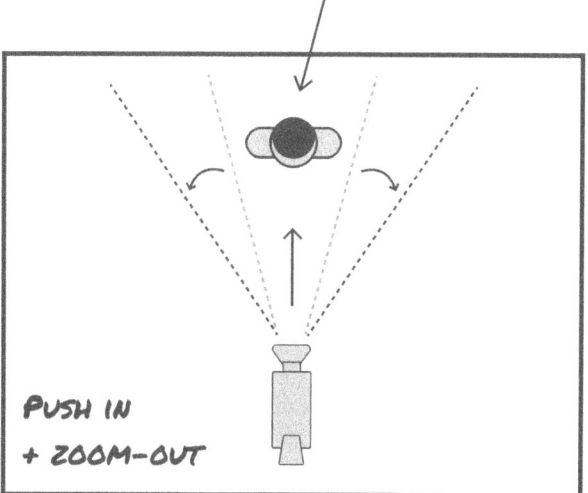

SHERIFF BRODY, REALIZING FOR THE FIRST TIME THERE IS A SHARK IN THE WATER

PUSH IN + ZOOM-OUT

The framing of a shot has its own terminology based on how much of the subject is shown. Each framing has its uses and conveys information to the audience about how a character is feeling, how they are situated in space relative to others and their environment, or the actions of key objects in a scene.

Extreme Close-Up (ECU)

MARY: "John, did you eat the last granola bar?"

Close-Up (CU)

JOHN - looking guilty:
"I may have."

Medium Shot (MS)

MARY: "We agreed to share it!"

Two-Shot (TS)

JOHN: "I know. I just...I was so hungry!"

Over-the-shoulder (OTS)

JOHN: "I'll...I'll buy you more!"

Wide Shot (WS)

MARY: "John..."

Extreme Wide Shot (EWS)

MARY: "How exactly do you intend to do that?"

YOUR TASK:

As we mentioned earlier, storyboards are a middle step between a screenplay and a motion picture. In this challenge, you will imagine a scene in the following script and then storyboard it on the next several pages:

INT. LAUNDROMAT - NIGHT

DELILAH is reading a book intently in front of a row of washing
machines. A nearby machine's barrel stops spinning, and an obnoxious
buzzer sounds. DELILAH gets up without taking her eyes off the book.

                            SAMSON
            Excuse me, I think you're unloading my clothes.

DELILAH looks at SAMSON. She looks at the pair of boxers she is
currently holding.

                            DELILIAH
              Ahh! I'm so sorry.

What a Concept: Story Flow

The basic structure of interactive stories is simple. They always have some kind of starting point, there may or may not be an endpoint, and there are always steps along the way, with choices that branch off and return. In designing narrative games and interactive fiction, creators often use some variation on a flow diagram, at least for prototyping.

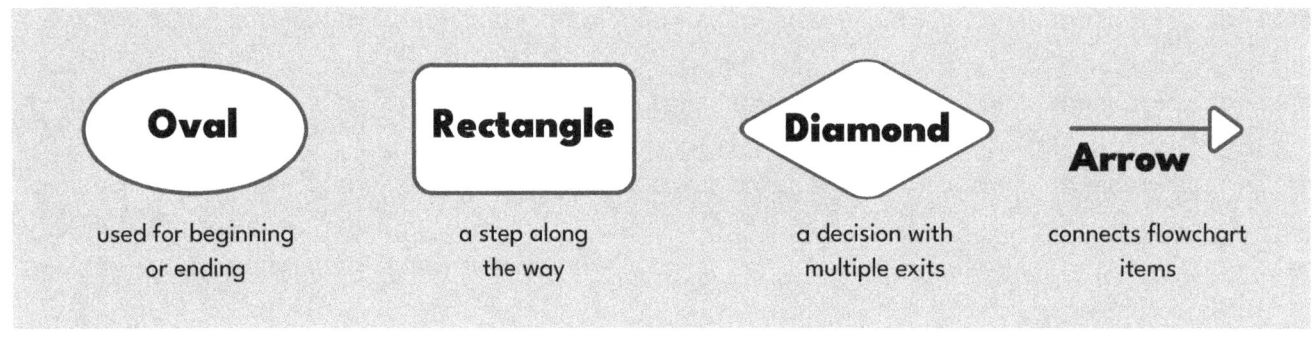

Oval used for beginning or ending

Rectangle a step along the way

Diamond a decision with multiple exits

Arrow connects flowchart items

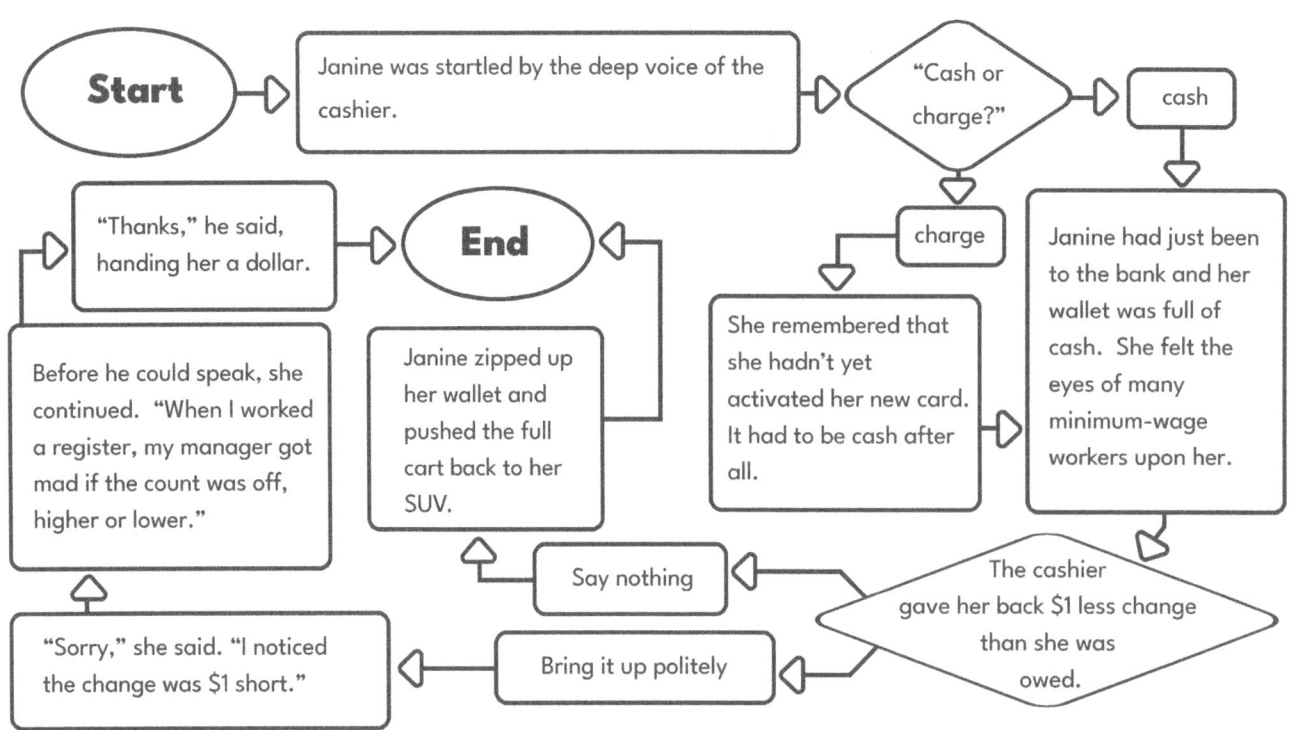

Notice how sometimes choices can merge back again, to keep consequences manageable. Janine chose "charge" but then remembered that she hadn't activated her new card. False choices like this are used often in games, both to control the outcome of a narrative but also to minimize writing entire other storylines.

Try writing your own interactive story flowchart here. We recommend you keep it very simple, like a brief conversation in an elevator.

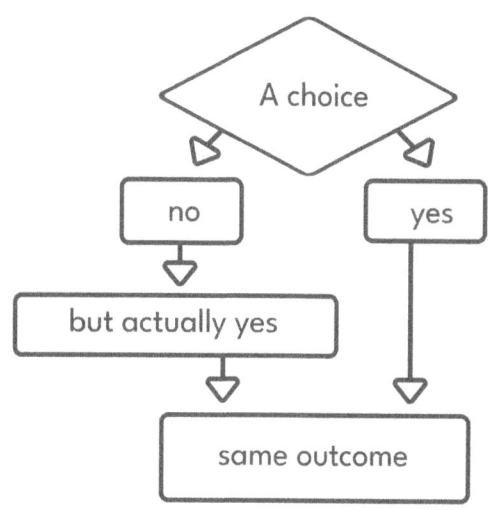

TRY IT OUT! Use this space to create a narrative flow.

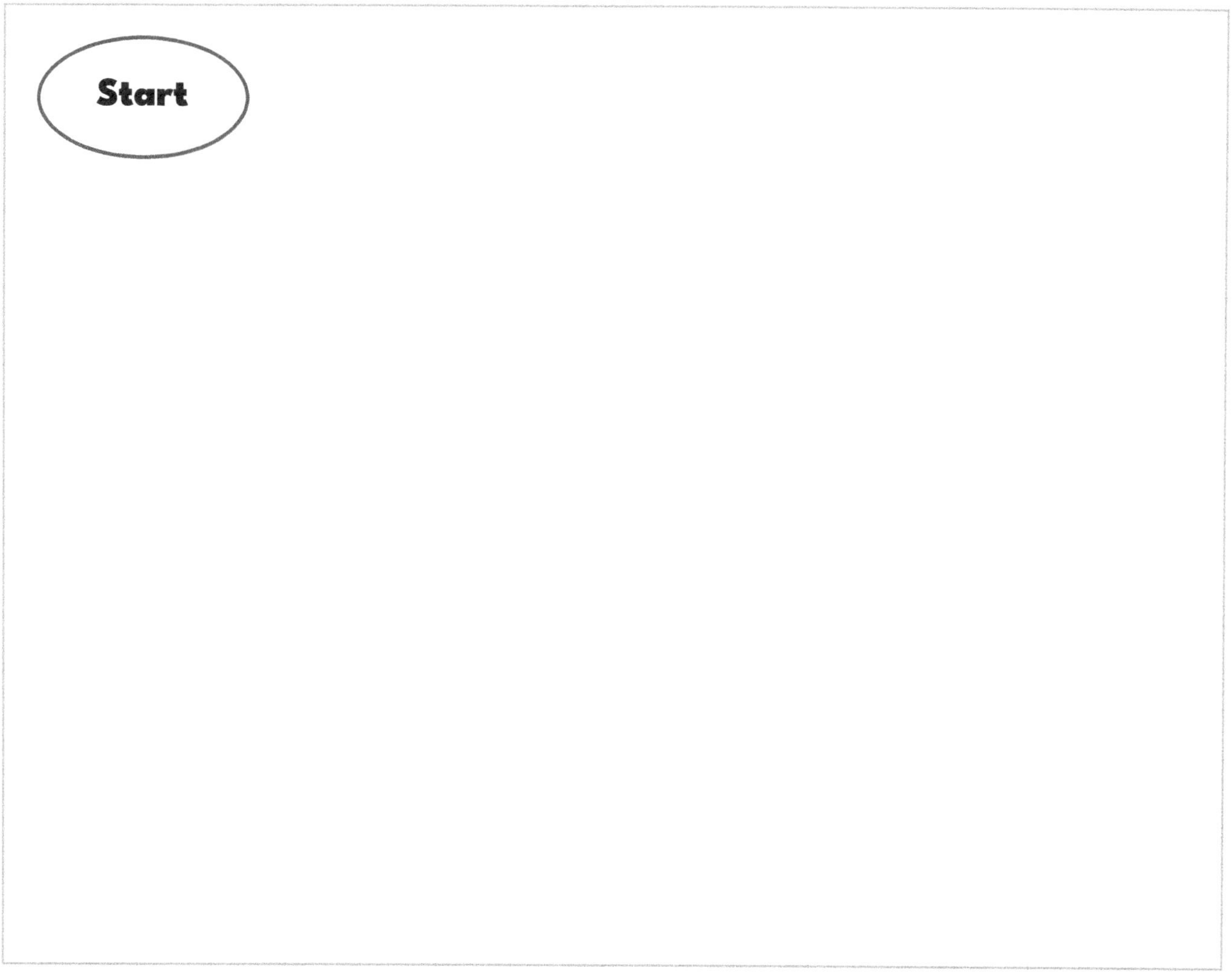

Start

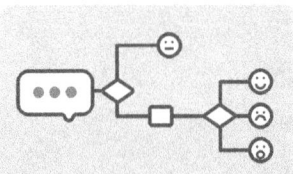

Narrative Design: Roll and Move

The following is the board for a simple roll-and-move game.

A Start	B	C	D	E	F

					G

M	L	K	J	I	H

N					

O	P	Q	R	S	T

The rules are:

1. One or more players start on space "A." They should read card "A" together.

2. Players take turns.

3. On each player's turn, they roll a single four-sided dice and move that many spaces forward (stopping at the end of the board when there are no more spaces left).

4. The player then reads the card marked with the same letter as the space they're on.

5. If the card has special instructions, they are followed.

6. Otherwise, the first player to read the card on the final space wins.

4 1
4 4
4 3
2 3
4 1
1 4
2 1
2 3
3 3
2 4
1 4
3 2
2 3
1 1
1 4
3 2
1 2
4 1
3 2
3 3
2 4

Your task is to write a card for each space on the board.

So, why is this a narrative design exercise? Well, this game should also be the story of a journey. Each card should tell a new part of that story. The story should be amusing enough that the single-player version of the game is still satisfying to play.

Each card can also have gameplay consequences. For example, here are a few cards you might write if this were a game about a trip to the grocery.

A You enter the grocery store, list in hand. You pull out a grocery cart with four functional wheels and begin.	**N** Looks like you forgot to turn the list over. There are more items on the back. **Go to B.**	**P** If you want to pick up some flowers for your partner, **go to Q.** Otherwise go directly **to R.**

As you write, you will want to playtest the game. Pay special attention to continuity. For instance, making references and callbacks to cards the player may have landed on previously can result in confusion if the player didn't land on those cards. It would also help to have an idea of how you want to handle branching dialogue. It would be a good idea to work through *What a Concept: Story Flow* on page 72 if you haven't already.

As usual, use the random numbers in the margin. Instead of using a game token, write a symbol in the space you land on, along with a number for which turn you're on. Use a different symbol for each playthrough. So on your first playthrough if you use a star symbol, you might have a space that looks like the one shown to the right.

> **B**
>
> *6

TRY IT OUT!

Use the following pages to write your cards. Some cards are left blank so they can be used for revisions of earlier cards. You may also want to add several variations of the same space to the board. If so, the player may choose the card they want to follow. Playtest early and often. Good luck!

2 3
2 1
3 2
2 4
3 4
4 4
1 1
3 1
3 4
2 4
2 3
1 2
3 1
3 1
4 4
2 1
2 3
1 2
3 4
4 4
1 3

A

B

C

D

E

F

G

H

I

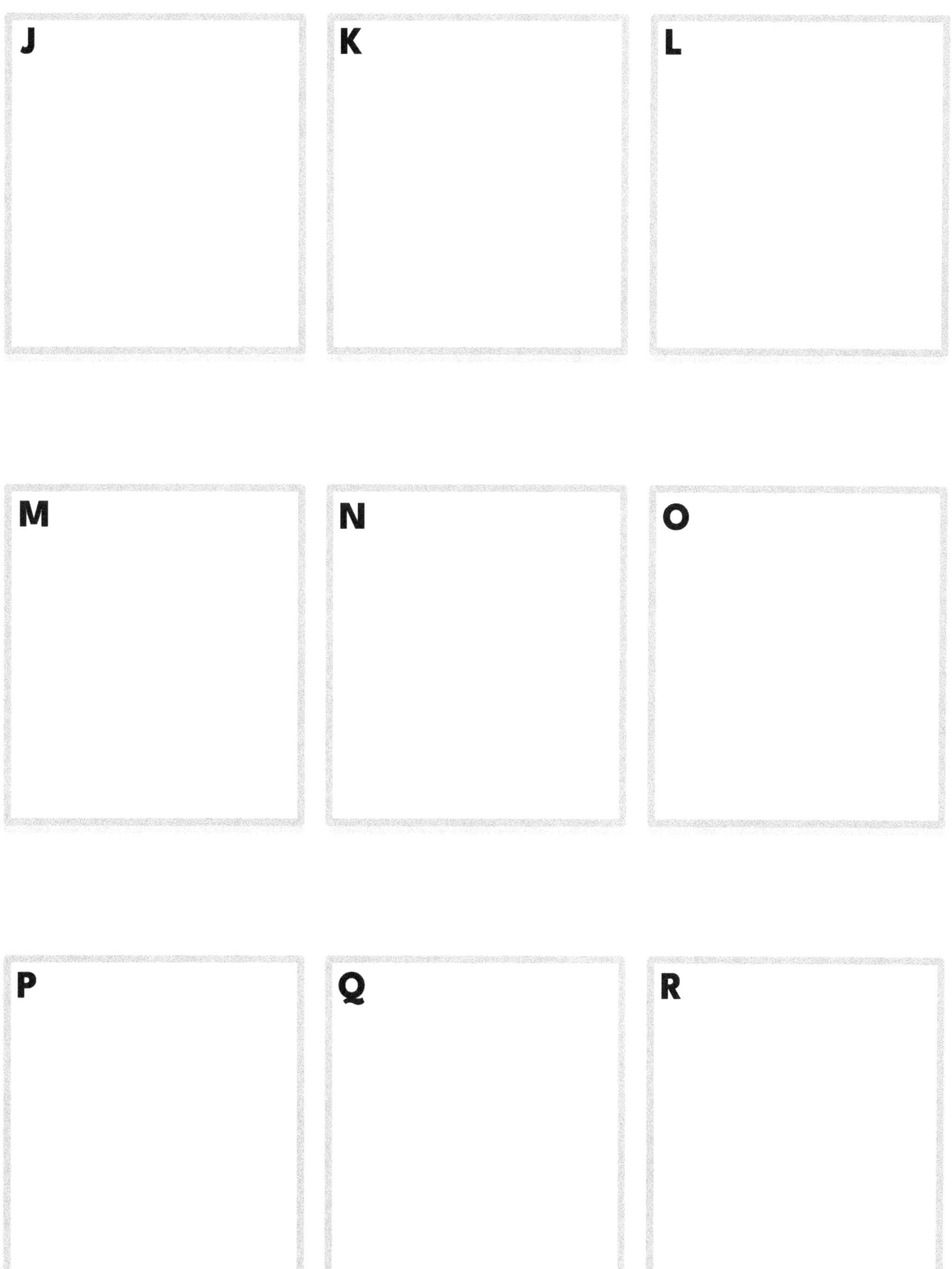

J

K

L

M

N

O

P

Q

R

S

T

Randomized Game Idea: Hidden Role

Pioneered by party games like *Mafia* and *Werewolf*, hidden role games have become a genre unto themselves, including classics like *Among Us* and *Secret Hitler*. The structure of these games essentially constitute a procedural narrative about keeping and discovering secrets. Let's randomly generate some parameters of a new hidden role game here, and use the following pages to construct a game from those parameters.

	A — Roles	B — Traitors' Goal	C — Loyals' Goal	D — Elimination
•	There is one hidden role: Traitor.	Traitors and accomplices win by sabotaging the Loyals' goal.	Loyals win by gathering all items from a board.	Players are eliminated by public vote between rounds.
••	There are two hidden roles: Traitor and Accomplice.	Traitors and Accomplices win by eliminating all Loyal players.	Loyals win by answering a certain number of trivia questions correctly.	Players are eliminated by blind vote between rounds.
•••	There are two hidden roles: Traitor and Anti-Traitor.	Traitors and Accomplices win by eliminating all Loyals, then accomplishing their goal themselves.	Loyals win by getting all sets of pair-matched cards in a memory game.	It costs three tokens to eliminate another player. Each player starts with 1 token.
•• ••	There are three hidden roles: Traitor, Accomplice, and Anti-Traitor.	Traitors and Accomplices win by sabotaging the Loyals' goal.	Loyals win by solving a puzzle one move at a time.	Players are eliminated by putting all votes in a bag and choosing blindly from the bag.
•• •• •	There are four hidden roles: Traitor, Accomplice, Anti-Traitor, Anti-Traitor's Assistant.	Traitors and Accomplices win by eliminating all Loyals.	Loyals win by collectively moving an object to a goal zone.	Players are eliminated by another player when it is that player's turn.
:: ::	Everyone gets a different role.	Traitors and Accomplices win by eliminating all Loyals, then accomplishing their goal themselves.	Loyals win by eliminating all Traitors and Accomplices.	Players are eliminated by decree of the player elected President.

Circle all randomly chosen parameters on the previous page.

Here and on the next page, create a fuller description (and any necessary sketches) of the game that's only hinted at by your random selections.

To help visualize the idea, here is a diagram of a group of eight people seated in a circle. Label each person with a name, a personality trait, and the role they've been randomly given. You can make it easier by representing real people from your life. Imagine how this playthrough will pan out, and make any adjustments to the design you feel are needed.

1 Name: _____
Personality Trait: _____
Role: _____

2 Name: _____
Personality Trait: _____
Role: _____

3 Name: _____
Personality Trait: _____
Role: _____

4 Name: _____
Personality Trait: _____
Role: _____

5 Name: _____
Personality Trait: _____
Role: _____

6 Name: _____
Personality Trait: _____
Role: _____

7 Name: _____
Personality Trait: _____
Role: _____

8 Name: _____
Personality Trait: _____
Role: _____

Breaking It Down: Anatomy of a Story

It's been theorized that there is an innate story-drive in human minds. Whether it's natural or a strangely universal product of culture, it's undeniable that humans cannot help but organize events into narrative. Bizarrely, there are similarities in our favorite stories even across cultures. There have been many attempts to catalog these shared elements. Propp's Morphology of the Folktale, Palmer & Howard's 36 Dramatic Situations, and Campbell's Hero's Journey are perhaps the best known.

At a basic level, stories always have a beginning, middle, and end, even if the order they're told in isn't straightforward. In the beginning we have exposition—the audience needs to get caught up on the characters, the setting, and the central conflict(s). Once conflict is established, the characters struggle against it, usually facing at least one setback. This is the middle of the story. Later, once the outcome of the struggle is clear (win, lose, or draw) we enter the end of the story. Then the audience learns the practical and emotional consequences, known as the denouement, and the story comes to a close. Not every story fits this pattern, which is called "three-act structure," but it's essentially the default.

Let's pick a story and break it down.

Cinderella

Beginning
- **Exposition:** Cinderella is a young woman who lives with her wicked stepmother and her two wicked stepsisters. They live in a kingdom with a prince who needs to choose a wife from among his subjects.
- **Introduction of the conflict:** The Prince announces that he will host a ball, to which all eligible women from the kingdom are invited, in order to find a suitable bride. Cinderella wants to go, but her wicked stepmother won't let her. Even if allowed, she doesn't have suitable clothing or travel.

Middle
- **Attempt to face the conflict:** Cinderella resigns herself to staying at home, but her Fairy Godmother appears and gives her a gown and a carriage, which will both expire at midnight. Cinderella goes to the ball and charms the Prince.
- **Setback:** Midnight approaches before Cinderella can introduce herself, and she must run back to

her carriage to avoid her clothes and carriage transforming before his eyes. As she flees she leaves behind a single glass slipper.

- **Recovery:** The Prince attempts to find the glass slipper's owner by traveling his kingdom to see whom it fits. The Wicked Stepmother attempts to conceal Cinderella and put her daughters forward, but the Prince and Cinderella are reunited.

End

- **Denouement:** Cinderella and the Prince are married, and we are promised they will live happily ever after.

TRY IT OUT!

Choose another story you know well and attempt to dissect it into these same bullet points.

> **Beginning**
> - Exposition
> - Introduction of the conflict
>
> **Middle**
> - Attempt to face the conflict
> - Setback
> - Recovery
>
> **End**
> - Denouement

Now it's time to reverse the process. Use these bullet points to craft an original story of your own. To keep things manageable, write a story with yourself or someone you know as the main character. For a main conflict, use a simple desire this person might have. For example, they might want to save up enough money for a used Chevy Equinox or to make a trip to White Castle.

TRY IT OUT!

Craft an original using these bullet points:

Beginning
- Exposition
- Introduction of the conflict

Middle
- Attempt to face the conflict
- Setback
- Recovery

End
- Denouement

Chapter Four

Sport

You miss 100% of the shots you don't take.

—Wayne Gretzky

—Michael Scott

—Eric Lang

Reflection: Rules Heavy and Light

Play can be defined as freedom of movement within a rigid structure. But how rigid is that structure, and how much freedom of movement is there, really? We are not the first to point out that games exist not on computers or playing cards, but in human minds. Consequently, games can be fun for players even if they are not fully specified—and perhaps even more so. There are classic games, like Monopoly, which intentionally leave some parameters open to house rules and rules lawyering. In tabletop RPGs, whose scope is so vast that a full ruleset could never be written, the duty of judgment is given to a game master. Even the early console games left scorekeeping to the player. That said, most computer and console games are fully specified, since by convention everything that is doable in a digital game is allowed.

Write about a positive experience with a game that left itself open to interpretation, or a negative experience with a game you feel was too rigid. How does this affect your perception of the way that "rules-light" games may suit a situation or a set of players?

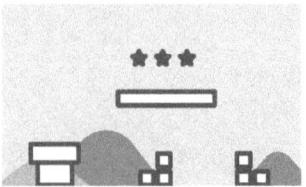

Level Design: Soccer/Football

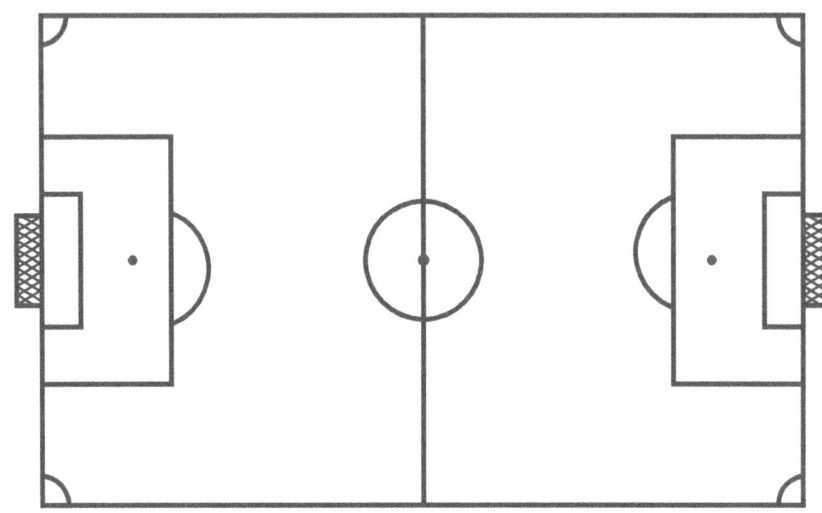

We're all familiar with the regulation soccer pitch—a big rectangle with goal nets sticking out on either side.

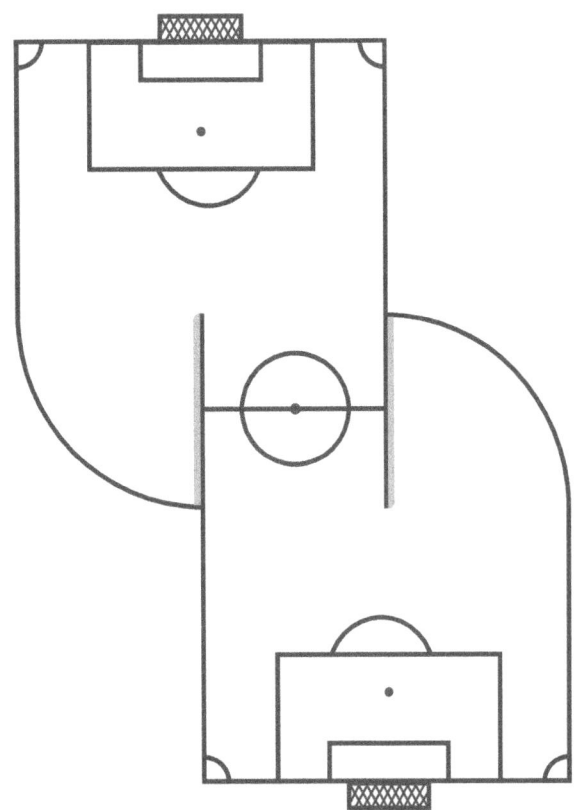

Let's spend some time brainstorming alternative shapes for the field. Try to make your new playfield designs allow for the same ruleset to be used. For instance, there must be a center circle where the kickoff takes place. There must also be a surrounding out-of-bounds area where players can stand when they toss the ball back into play or do corner kicks.

Think three-dimensionally! Here's an example to the left.

Some questions to spark ideas:

- Do there have to be just two goals?
- Does the field need to be one continuous area?
- Can you make the playfield fair without making it symmetrical?

TRY IT OUT!

Sketch your field designs here and on the following page. Use the grid section if you need something more precise:

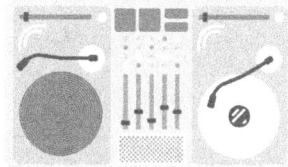

Remix: Basketball

In considering this section of the book, you might be questioning the utility of learning about the design of sports. Most popular sports are the product of a long and undirected evolutionary process, rather than the concerted efforts of designers. That's not true of basketball, which was created by a single man, James Naismith. Let's build upon his work, here.

The Basic and Abridged Rules of Basketball:

1. Two teams of five people compete.
2. The game takes place on a wood-floored rectangular "court" with elevated horizontal hoops (or "baskets") on either end. Each basket is designated as a goal for the team that starts on the side of the court opposite it.
3. The game is split into four quarters, each having 8-12 minutes of playtime. The clock is paused when the ball is not in play.
4. A single rigid bouncy ball is used. It must be held by players in their hands.
5. Play begins when the ball is tossed into the center of court by the referee.
6. The goal is to put the ball through their designated hoop from the top (thus "scoring a basket"). This is worth 2 points if done from within a designated arc 6-8 meters from the goal, or 3 points from outside.
7. After each basket, a member of the non-scoring team is given the ball and must re-enter the game from their side of the court.
8. Players can move the ball across the court by tossing it or by holding it but cannot move more than two steps with the ball unless they bounce the ball on the floor.
9. No intentional contact is allowed between players.
10. When time has expired for all four quarters, the winner is the team with the most points.

CHOOSE ONE RULE TO CHANGE (OR ADD!) THAT YOU THINK MIGHT IMPROVE THE GAME OF BASKETBALL:

What do you think would be the consequences of changing the rule as you describe?

Remember that basketball is not just a game for the players; it's also a spectator sport.
How do you think your new rule might affect the watchability of basketball?

Randomized Game Idea: Sport

Read on for instructions on how to use the following grid.

	A Teams	**B** Arena	**C** Score Points By	**D** The Catch
•	One-on-one	On an open field 100 meters by 75	Moving a thing into a designated area	But players can only use specific parts of their bodies
••	Two teams of two	On a strip of hard surface only 1.5m wide	Touching a player on the opponent's team in a certain way	But players can only use a specific tool
•••	Two teams of 4–10	In a dirt circle 6m across	Stealing something from the opponent	But players cannot move more than two steps without doing something
::	Four players competing individually	On a hard surface 23m by 8m, bisected by a net	Pushing an opposing player (literally or figuratively) out of bounds	But players must ride on an animal or machine
:::	Two teams of four, each player has an animal companion	In an Olympic-sized pool	Hitting a target	But some players are blindfolded
::::	Two teams of 11–25	In an arena filled with obstacles	Rendering an opponent immobile	But players must stay within a specific zone

Use the dice to select one rule from each column. These rules are more vague than ever, so you'll need to fill in the gaps to create a new sport of your own.

WRITE YOUR NEW GAME RULES HERE:

Breaking It Down: Playground Games

This exercise is about identifying elements of popular equipment-free playground games and then recombining those elements into a new playground game of your own.

Let's start by listing some playground games that fit into this category:

- Tag
- Freeze Tag
- Red Rover
- Blob
- Hide and Seek
- Sardines
- Duck Duck Goose
- Simon Says
- Red Light, Green Light
- Mother, May I?
- Murder Handshake
- Thumbs Up
- Thumb War
- Ghost in the Graveyard

If you know these games, you may have already noticed some elements in common.
If there are any you aren't familiar with, please look up the rules.

First, make a list of the elements of equipment-less playground games. The first few are done for you to give you a sense of the granularity we're looking for.

1. TOUCH ANOTHER PLAYER AGAINST THEIR WILL

2. LINK ARMS TO FORM A GROUP

3.

4.

5.

6.

7.

8.

9.

10.

11.

12.

Now that you have your building blocks, use the following space to try to recombine some of them into a new equipment-free playground game.

Keep your audience in mind! The rules must be simple enough for a bunch of five-year-olds and should accommodate a wide range of player counts.

Cross-Training: Toy Design

At the heart of many great games is a toy. For most sports, it's a ball. For any first-person shooter, it's a virtual gun. In a car race, it's the car itself. It's almost certain that toys came before games, and there's still a lot we can learn about the ways they foster open-ended play.

Toy designers often categorize play into "play patterns."

An incomplete list of play patterns:

Play Pattern	Example
Occupational Role-Play	Pretend to Own a Pizza Parlor
Caretaking Role-Play	Baby Doll, Hospital
Ritual Play	Hand-slapping patterns, Cat's Cradle
Kinetic Cooperative Play	Double Dutch, Keepy-Uppy, Catch
Kinetic Competitive Play	Jumping Contest, Bloody Knuckles
Combat Role-Play	Cops and Robbers
Proxy Role-Play	Dolls, Action Figures
Musical Play	Toy Instruments
Art Play	Finger Paints
Aesthetic Play	Styling Hair, Decorating Notebooks
Construction Play	Lego, Lincoln Logs
Collection Play	Sorting Coins, Collecting Seashells
Performance Play	Karaoke, Puppet Theater
Dexterity Play	Block Towers, Marbles

YOUR TASK:

Choose two play patterns from the list. On the next few pages design a physical toy that is intended to encourage both forms of play.

Marvin Glass, legendary toy design guru, formulated these 10 questions for assessing a toy design:

1. Does the toy give a child an active role?
2. Does it allow inventive play?
3. Is it sturdy enough to take rough play?
4. Is it easy to understand?
5. Is it easy to use?
6. Is it pleasant to touch?
7. Does it allow for playing together?
8. Will it challenge a child either mentally, or physically, or both?
9. Can children use it to explore adult work patterns realistically?
10. Will it give a child a sense of discovery or self-expression?

Glass believed that the quality of a toy depended on how many of these questions it could answer affirmatively.

| 5–6: probably a good toy | 7–8: commendable | 9–10: the idea is excellent |

Keep these criteria in mind as you design your toy.*

*If you haven't done the exercise **Cross-Training: Schematic Drawing**, it may be useful to you.

Chapter Five

Word Games

I do the *New York Times* crossword puzzle every morning to keep the old gray matter ticking.

—Carol Burnett

Reflection: Serious Games

There is an ongoing discussion in game design circles about using games to create a change in the player. One could say that any work of art is capable of altering the mind of its audience, but the question is whether games can accomplish real-world goals in a direct and measurable sense.

Here are several ways game creators try to do this:
- Educational games try to bring their player closer to a learning goal, by increasing either their knowledge, their skill, or their interest in a topic.
- Persuasive games put forth some sort of position on real-world issues and use the game as an argument in defense of that position.
- Behavior change games seek to improve the life of their players by helping them to create new habits, break old ones, or recontextualize and reflect on their behavior.
- Wellness games have a direct, positive effect on the physiology of their players. A few are even approved for clinical use by the US FDA.
- Citizen science games use the puzzle-solving and information-gathering abilities of large collections of players to create new publishable knowledge.

Do you feel that games should be instrumentalized by society in these ways?
Why or why not?

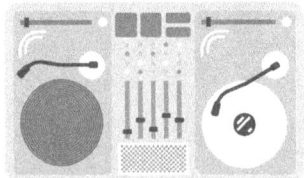

Remix: Word Scramble

The classic word-scramble game, whose name we all know, has a very particular board layout and set of letter tiles. The board, for example, has a star in the exact center, indicating where the first letter of the first word must be placed. It also has the following rules (among others):

1. Two to four players...

2. take turns...

3. drawing letters randomly from a bag...

4. into a seven-letter "hand," which is replenished after every turn.

5. On their turn, each player attempts to place a word on the board, or to extend an existing word (or words), by placing letter tiles from their hand into empty spaces on the board.

6. New letter tiles placed on the board must be cardinally adjacent to at least one previously placed tile (or start on the star, if it's the first word).

7. Words can be formed only left-to-right or top-to-bottom. Never both, and never non-contiguously.

8. A move that produces any non-word letter sequence is illegal and cannot be played.

9. Each move is scored by adding the letter totals of tiles involved in the word (or words) produced, even if they were not placed this turn.

10. Letter or word score multiplier spaces can be found around the board. These modify the score only if a tile was placed on that space this turn. Multipliers are: triple word score (Wx3), double word score (Wx2), triple letter score (Lx3), and double letter score (Lx2).

11. Play proceeds until the tile bag is no longer able to fill a player's hand.

12. Highest total score wins.

NOW GIVE IT A SHOT

Start by playing a sample game against yourself on the miniature board supplied. Since you'll know both players' hands, don't try to play defensively—just make the best words you can each turn. Draw tiles by skipping a random number of tiles from 1 to 10 and then drawing in order thereafter. Cross off tiles as you use them. Continue until no tiles remain.

Player 1

Score:

Player 2

Score:

Next, choose a single rule from the list of 12 word-scramble rules to change in order to make the game better. Write your new version of that rule here. Then, try playing a round against yourself using this new rule.

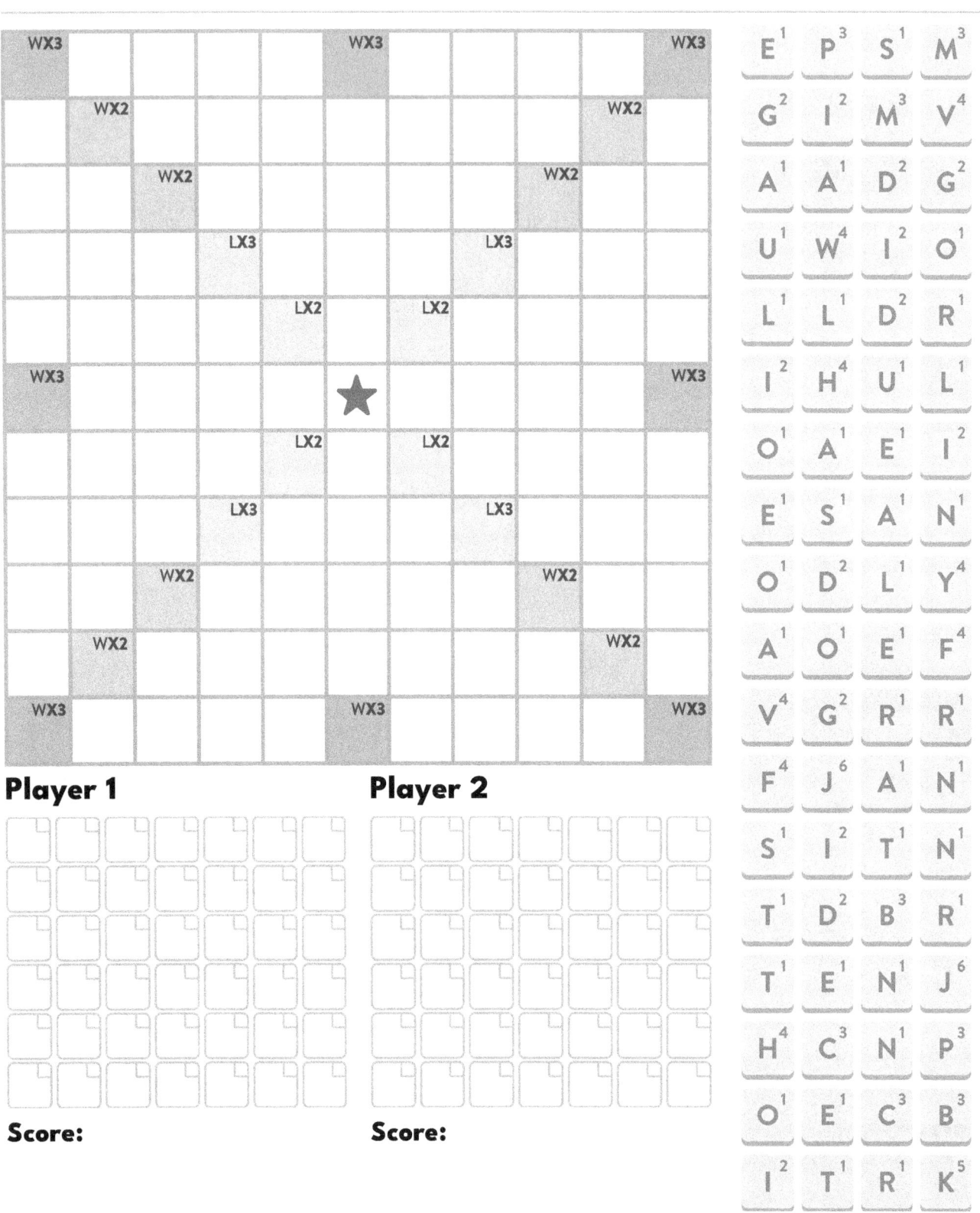

Player 1

Player 2

Score:

Score:

Finally, consider, did your new version of the rule have the desired result? Here's another chance. You can write another version of the same rule here, *or* you can try changing another rule to better support the first change (or both).

___

Letter tiles:

D^2 S^1 O^1 L^1
N^1 I^2 J^6 I^2
O^1 V^4 L^1 S^1
E^1 I^2 I^2 U^1
D^2 L^1 P^3 R^1
R^1 V^4 T^1 A^1
W^4 L^1 N^1 E^1
I^2 A^1 R^1 E^1
Y^4 N^1 P^3 F^4
B^3 R^1 U^1 A^1
B^3 A^1 C^3 G^2
F^4 I^2 E^1 A^1
G^2 O^1 N^1 D^2
S^1 A^1 C^3 T^1
K^5 M^3 H^4 H^4
N^1 E^1 O^1 T^1
G^2 D^2 E^1 R^1
M^3 O^1 T^1 J^6

Player 1

Score:

Player 2

Score:

Level Design: Crossword Puzzle

A crossword puzzle is an art form in itself, combining trivia, vocabulary, and spatial problem-solving. Players must fill in a grid with one letter in each blank square such that the contiguous words or phrases match a given clue. If you've never done a crossword puzzle, you'll understand after we show a small example.

When you've filled in the blanks completely, check your work against the following answer key.

Notice that because solvers get additional information from intersecting words, and from the number of letters needed to fill the space, the clues do not necessarily need to be unambiguous on their own. For example, DOWN 4, which is "one and _____", could perhaps be "the same" or "done" or "only," but only the last solution fits the space and the letters from other clues.

The addition of black spaces on the grid gives the puzzle-maker more freedom to choose places in the grid where discontinuity allows them to avoid awkward conflicts where clues intersect.

Truly masterful crossword puzzles also connect their solutions thematically, giving the solvers another dimension of context and affording the clues themselves to get even less specific.

ACROSS

1. in addition
5. circus jokester
6. big-budget videogame
7. one earth spin

DOWN

1. in the style of
2. fill
3. bottom left on compass, abbr.
4. one and _____
5. where circus jokesters emerge

Next, you'll try your hand at making a crossword puzzle of your own. Start by making the solution grid on the left and blacking out all the unused squares.

TIP: This is the toughest part. Use a pencil and expect a few false starts.

Next, mark the squares where new words begin by numbering their top-left corners sequentially, starting from the top left of the grid and proceeding in reading order—left-to-right and top-to-bottom. Copy the numbers and the blacked-out squares to the grid to the right. This is the puzzle grid.

The Curse of Knowledge

Studies have shown that once a person knows something, it becomes very difficult to imagine not knowing it. How does this apply to puzzle-making? Generally, clues will be more difficult than you think they are. Try to adjust accordingly, and ideally test your puzzles on others.

Now let's write some clues. As you saw, they're divided into sections: Across and Down. Clues should be a mix of different levels of obscurity, with the understanding that the easier clues will give solvers more information to get the harder ones.

Across

Down

Stepping It Up

Now that you've made your first crossword puzzle, it's time to step up your game. First we'll need you to choose a theme—something broad and familiar like movies or food. You'll also have a bigger grid to work with. Try to fill it, as much as possible, with words or phrases associated with your theme.

The Theme: _____

SOLUTION HERE

PUZZLE HERE

Across

Down

Randomized Game Idea: Word Game

A	B	C	D
Players	**Materials**	**The Object**	**The Twist**
A solitaire game	Using pencil and paper	Make the most words	Letters can be stolen
Four players in teams of two	Using dice with letters on the sides	Make the longest words	You can't use some letters until you "free" them
Two to four players, each in competition with the rest	Using square letter tiles	Make the highest-scoring words	Words need to fit a theme
Two to four players all cooperating	Using a deck of letter cards	Be the last player with letters remaining	Some spaces only accept certain letters
Two to four players all playing against a single mastermind player	Using a giant mat of letters players can stand on	Be the first player to use up your letters	A root word can only be used once
A casual party game for five or more	Using alphabet refrigerator magnets	Fill in the space given with valid words	Your letters can be rearranged to form another word

Use the dice to select one rule from each column. These rules are more vague than ever, so you'll need to fill in the gaps.

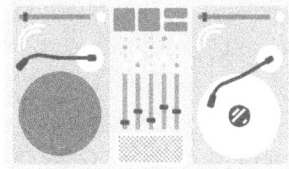

Remix: Hangman

The Rules of Hangman:

1. One player acts as the game-master, with one or more other players acting as guessers.

2. The game is played on a writing surface visible to all players.

3. A stick-figure gallows is drawn on the surface.

4. The game-master chooses a word or phrase that the guessers must try to guess.

5. The game-master draws underlines for each letter of the word or phrase, leaving gaps for spaces between words where appropriate.

6. The game-master draws a designated area for incorrectly guessed letters.

7. Guessers take turns choosing a letter they think might be part of the phrase.

   a. If the letter is present in the phrase, the game-master must write the letter above every underline corresponding to each place where the letter appears in the phrase.

   b. If the letter is not present, the game-master draws a body part of a "hanged man" beneath the gallows and adds the letter to the incorrect letter area to keep track.

8. If the game-master draws a complete person being hanged, the guessers lose.

9. If the guessers are able to fill in all the underlined letters, or guess the phrase early, they win.

As you can see, Hangman is a very loose and underspecified game. Many aspects are left to the discretion of the game-master. For instance, "When are guessers allowed to guess the whole phrase, and how often?" and "How many body parts are required to make a hanged man?"

Start by playing a round of the normal game. Since it's hard to imagine not knowing the phrase to be guessed, use the list of letter guesses given (and don't look at the guesses until you've already chosen your phrase). Stop the game when you think a reasonable person would be able to guess the phrase from the letters showing or if your complete hanged man has been drawn.

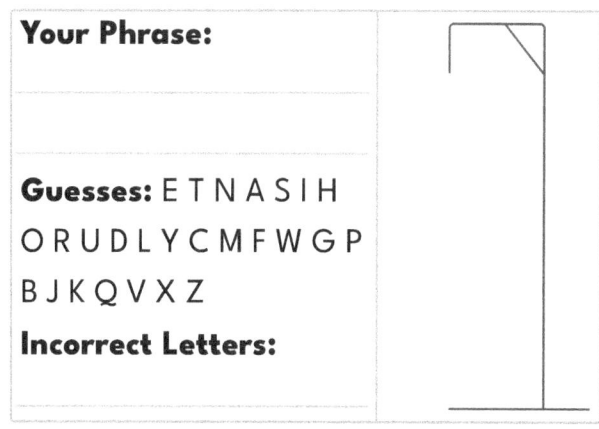

Your Phrase:

Guesses: E T N A S I H
O R U D L Y C M F W G P
B J K Q V X Z

Incorrect Letters:

Your task is to choose a rule other than the two locked rules (2 and 3) from the list and alter it to try to improve the game, while keeping to the spirit of hangman.

Your Revised Rule:

Your Phrase:

Guesses: R S T L N E H A V O W I M P Y G U M B F Z C D K J Q X

Incorrect Letters:

Feel free to change as many rules as necessary to support your new variant, including the one you changed before.

Your Phrase:

Guesses: A R O S E L I N T Y C H U M P D F G W B K J Z X Q V

Incorrect Letters:

Level Design: Word Find

A word find may not seem like a challenging domain within game design, but it is a reasonable microcosm of all puzzle-level design. Consider the difference in difficulty and fun between the following two word finds:

S	H	I	R	T
H	K	C	O	I
O	C	I	C	E
E	O	O	R	T
T	S	H	A	T

Find: shirt, tie, sock, shoe, hat, skirt

B	E	L	L	T
E	B	T	B	L
L	E	E	E	L
B	L	T	L	E
T	E	E	L	B

Find: belt

Let's start simple. Create your own 5x5 word find of your own. Start with a theme that will include lots of short words.

Theme:

Now make a list of words, five letters long or fewer, that fit the theme. Try to choose words that have some letters in common so they can occupy the same space on a small board.

List of Words:

Now arrange the words on this grid and fill in the remaining empty spaces with letters. You can make it easier by using filler letters that don't appear in your words. You can make it harder by using sequences of letters that create red herrings.

Great! Now try some alternative grids.

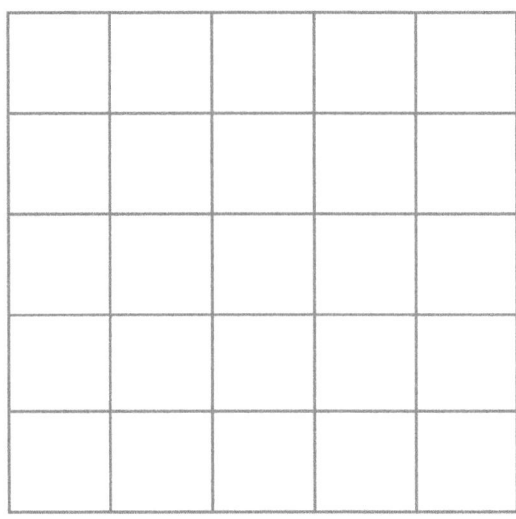

Theme:

List of Words:

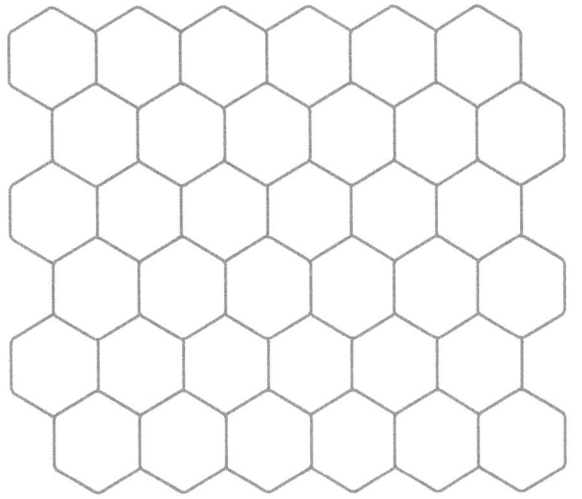

Notice that on this hex grid instead of eight neighbors, each space now has only six neighbors.

Theme:

List of Words:

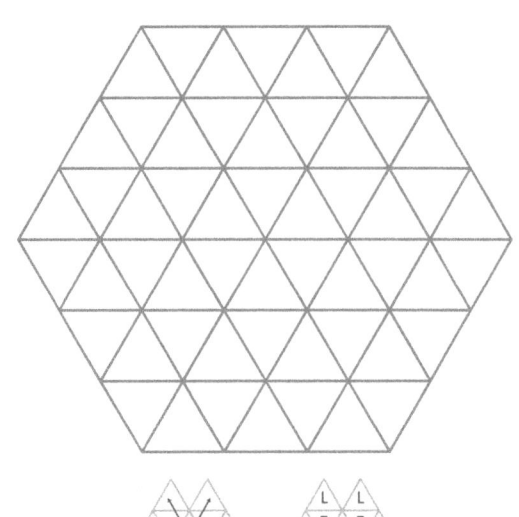

Here each letter has only three neighbors, but there are still six directions words can proceed in.

Want to make more? Here are some more grids for you to use. Also, be sure to double-check your grid in case you unitentionally made some innapropriate words.

Theme:

List of Words:

Theme:

List of Words:

What a Concept: Chain Reactions

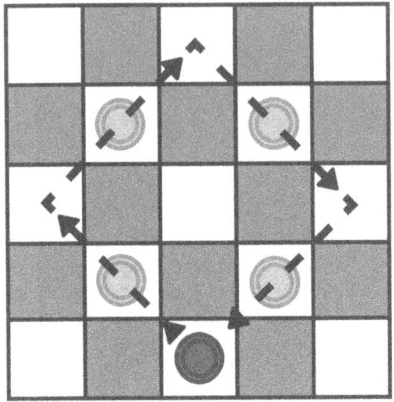

A chain reaction is a situation where a single in-game action can have the same effect as taking multiple actions would have. Like dominos, a move that triggers a chain reaction can create consequences that themselves create consequences, etc. For instance, in checkers, players can capture multiple pieces if they are arranged correctly.

Most match-three games, like *Bejeweled*, have ways of generating chain reactions of matches.

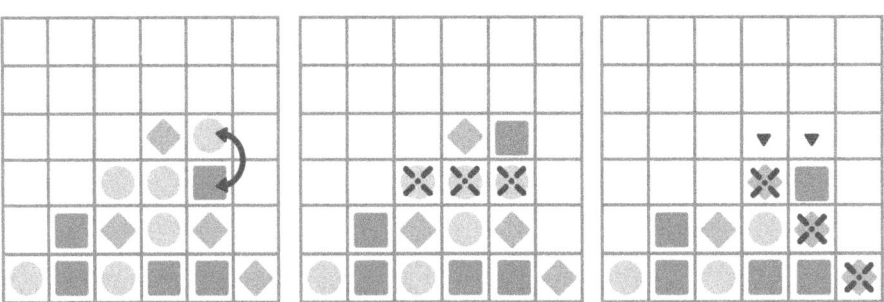

Chain reactions are an enviable feature for any game, as long as they don't exacerbate a first-mover advantage. There's a principle that every interaction the player has with a game should be amplified and returned as a way of rewarding them for their attention. Chain reactions are an excellent way of accomplishing this. Chain reactions also provide a route, without rubber-banding,[1] for dramatic comebacks.

On the following pages, you'll design a solitaire game for a standard set of playing cards, which allows the player to set up chain reactions. To give you an idea to get started, what would happen if you took cues from a card game like Uno or war, which are all about chain reactions, and applied it to your game?

---

[1] Rubber-banding, aka catch-up mechanic, is a way of keeping a game competitive if the difference in status between players becomes too great.

TRY IT!

Use the spaces on the next two pages to design your new game.
The decks are already shuffled, so feel free to use the cards in the order they are presented.

A♦	6♠	6♣	9♥
5♥	2♥	4♠	3♥
Q♠	10♥	8♦	K♠
K♦	8♣	Q♥	7♠
J♣	J♦	7♥	8♥
3♠	10♠	6♦	K♣
2♦	5♠	J♥	5♦
8♠	K♥	A♠	7♣
7♦	A♥	6♥	5♣
3♠	4♣	3♦	Q♣
9♦	9♣	2♣	Q♦
10♦	A♣	10♣	9♠
2♠	4♥	4♦	J♠

♥ 5	♥ 6	♦ 3	♦ K
♠ 4	♦ 6	♣ 5	♥ 7
♦ J	♥ J	♠ 10	♣ 10
♥ 9	♠ 9	♥ Q	♣ J
♠ 8	♠ A	♣ 4	♥ 8
♠ 6	♣ 8	♥ A	♠ J
♦ 9	♠ K	♠ 7	♦ 5
♦ A	♠ 3	♠ Q	♥ K
♦ 7	♠ 2	♥ 10	♥ 4
♣ 9	♣ 6	♣ 7	♦ 8
♠ 5	♣ Q	♠ 2	♣ A
♥ 3	♣ 2	♦ 10	♣ K
♦ 4	♥ 2	♣ 3	♦ Q

Chapter Six

Quantitative

The true spirit of delight, the exaltation, the sense of being more than Man, which is the touchstone of the highest excellence, is to be found in mathematics as surely as in poetry.

—Bertrand Russell

Reflection: Player Feedback

When in the course of game development it becomes necessary to gather feedback from people with no prior experience of your game, there are a few ways to accomplish it:

- Surveys (asking players to fill out a survey after playing)
- Live playtesting (watching one or more people playing your game)
  - with the target demographic
  - with a proxy
- Analytics (automated collection of player behavior data)

Surveys contain the least information but have the most formal status. They can be useful for evidence in a research setting or anywhere you need a lot of rigor. Live playtesting is usually the most informative but takes a lot of skill to interpret. Analytics gives you a firehose of information about what players are doing but not an inkling of why.

Watching new players struggle with your game (literally or figuratively) can be a painful process, as every flaw in your own model of player behavior is laid bare, and every misapprehension twists your heartstrings into knots. It can become very tempting to intervene during a play session and decrease the validity of the experiment or, even worse, to react defensively to negative responses.

It's wise rather to embrace the value of playtest for what it is: a method to make your game better, not a process of attacking your ideas. If problems in your game aren't fixed at this stage, it will be harder (and much more expensive) to fix the further into production you get.

While we're in the process of setting our ego aside, let's take it a step further. Players are often very good at blaming themselves for a problem in a game. They may use language like "I'm not good at strategy games" or "I'm terrible at staying focused, and I distract easily." While statements like that may be true, it is often a player's way of softening the blow of whatever criticism of your game is about to come next. It is likely that the problem is not them, but a flaw in your game.

Analytics are the impersonal data a digital game can gather about how players behave within it. Basic information like how long a level takes to complete, which solutions are most popular, and when they choose to stop playing (for the day, or forever) can have a huge impact on future iterations of your game. But even analytics can be deceptive. For instance, it is often hard to determine by behavior data alone whether players find an area frustrating and are trying everything just to proceed or are testing boundaries and experimenting because they are enjoying themselves.

There is one piece of wisdom that all professionals can agree upon: player feedback is the process of identifying problems, and not solutions. If a solution is suggested while gathering player feedback, either by the player themselves or by your own mind, it's wise to be very suspicious of that solution.

Take some time to consider how you plan to gather and use playtest feedback in your own work. How will you create an environment that best exposes your game's flaws and encourages playtesters to voice them? Also, consider how you'll react to trends you see in analytics data.

Cross-Training: Probability

Game designers use bounded randomness to create variability for their players, but we also need to understand the consequences of particular choices about that randomness. Unfortunately, that involves a particularly unpleasant branch of mathematics called probability and statistics.

Let's start with the most basic case: the probability of an isolated event from a class of equally probable events. The classic example is rolling a dice. If the dice is fair and six-sided, the probability of rolling any given number is 1/6.

How about the probability of drawing an ace of hearts from a deck of standard playing cards?

To get to the probability of one event **OR** another, you can add the individual probabilities. The probability of rolling a 5 or 6 is 1/6 + 1/6 = 2/6 = ⅓. What is the probability of drawing a king? K(hearts) + K(spades) + K(clubs) + K(diamonds) = 1/52 + 1/52 + 1/52 + 1/52 = 4/52 = 1/13.

What is the probability of drawing a face card?

It's rare that an event is considered in isolation like this. Often, we need to know the probability of a compound event, such as rolling two six-sided dice and their sum being 7.

The most intuitive way is to list all of the possibilities.

1st Roll	2nd Roll	Sum	1st Roll	2nd Roll	Sum	1st Roll	2nd Roll	Sum
1	1	2	3	1	4	5	1	6
1	2	3	3	2	5	5	2	7
1	3	4	3	3	6	5	3	8
1	4	5	3	4	7	5	4	9
1	5	6	3	5	8	5	5	10
1	6	7	3	6	9	5	6	11
2	1	3	4	1	5	6	1	7
2	2	4	4	2	6	6	2	8
2	3	5	4	3	7	6	3	9
2	4	6	4	4	8	6	4	10
2	5	7	4	5	9	6	5	11
2	6	8	4	6	10	6	6	12

Of 36 possibilities, 6 of them sum to 7, meaning the probability is 6/36 = 1/6.

What about the probability of rolling a total of 5 on three four-sided dice? Can you find some shortcuts to listing all 64 possibilities?

Some probability is conditional on events that come before. A simple case would be something like drawing an ace from a deck when another (unknown) card has already been drawn. Again, we list the possibilities, but this time they're not equally likely.

1st card was ace 4/52	**AND**	2nd card is ace 3/51

1st card was NOT ace 48/52	**AND**	2nd card is ace 4/51

AND relationships become multiplication, which gives us:

$$\left(\frac{4}{52} \times \frac{3}{51} \right) + \left(\frac{48}{52} \times \frac{4}{51} \right) = \frac{1}{221} + \frac{16}{221} = \frac{17}{221} = \frac{1}{13}$$

That's the same probability as simply drawing an ace from a full deck! What gives? Well, you can ask the same question another way. What is the probability that the second card in a deck is an ace?

So, while counting the probabilities of all possible outcomes is the surest way to get the right answer, one can often find shortcuts by transforming the problem in some way.

What is the probability of drawing two cards with the same value (A,2,3,4,5,6,7,8,9,10,J,Q,K) but different suits?

Another useful concept for this task is "expected value." Expected value is the sum of all outcome values multiplied by their probability. So the expected value of flipping a coin with sides 0 and 1 is 0.5. The expected value of flipping two coins is shown to the right.

Value	Probability
0	1/4
1	2/4
2	1/4

0 x 1/4 + 1 x 2/4 + 2 x 1/4 = ①

Now that you have a grasp of probability, I want you to invent a new two-player dice game that is completely fair but where the players do not have the same set of dice. Assume dice can have any number of sides, as long as they are integers (counting numbers) 2 or greater. The same dice cannot be used more than once in a turn. Players must decide (within limits you set) which dice to roll, and when. Describe your game and then demonstrate with calculations that with good decision-making it should be equally likely for either player to win.

A trivial example would be a game where two players simply face off. One player tosses four coins. The other player rolls a single four-sided dice ("d4") and subtracts 0.5 from the result.

Player	Value	Probability	Expected Value
A	0	1/16	
A	1	4/16	
A	2	6/16	2
A	3	4/16	
A	4	1/16	
B	0.5	1/4	
B	1.5	1/4	
B	2.5	1/4	2
B	3.5	1/4	

This is fair but is a pretty boring game. Let's see if you can do better!

What a Concept: Emergence

Emergence refers to the complex or surprising behavior that arises from a system with simple parts. In complexity science, the different types of system behaviors are separated into classes:

Class 1: Simple

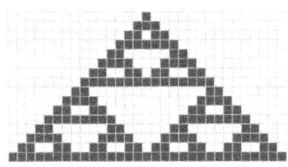

Class 2: Recursive

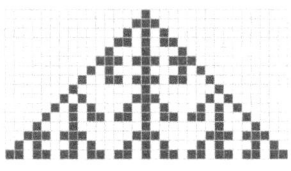

Class 4: Complex

Class 3: Chaotic

Confusingly, the order of ascending complexity is not the same as the order of their numbering. The point is that while recursive (aka fractal) behavior can be interesting, it's never surprising. And while chaos is always surprising, it's never interesting. Class-four systems have both, which is what makes them so desirable for game systems. In fact, computers themselves fall into class four.

One of the simplest supersets of systems that exhibits all four types of behavior is one-dimensional cellular automata. These are lines of cells that start at some given initial condition, and each subsequent state is determined by a simple rule that takes into account the previous state of the cell and its neighbors. For instance, the following is one rule (Wolfram code 73):

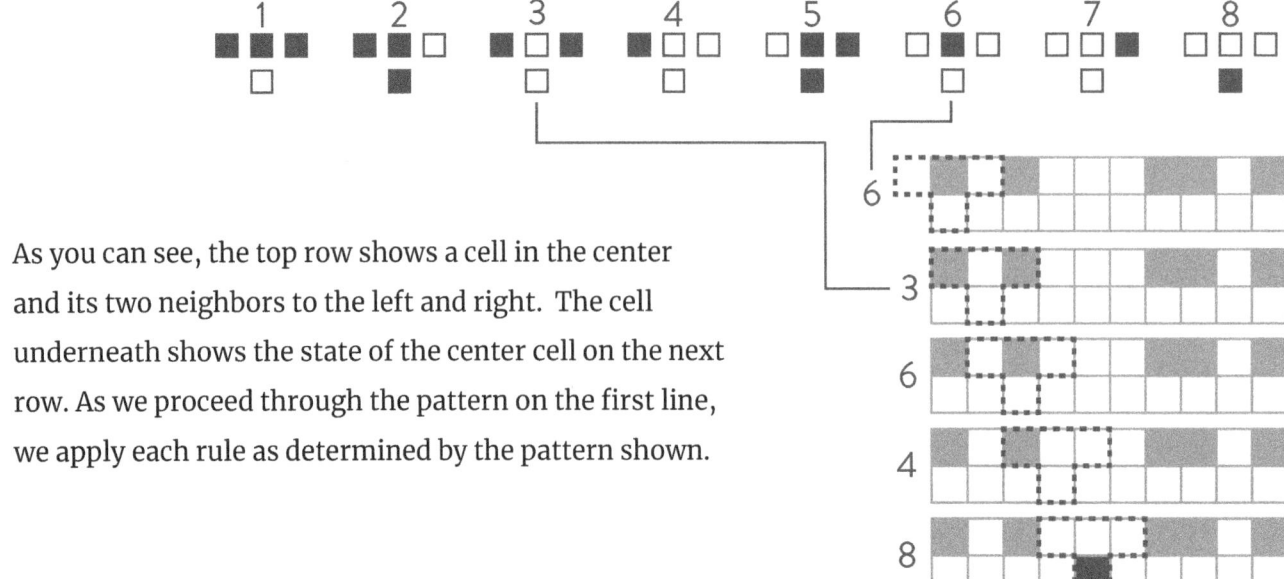

As you can see, the top row shows a cell in the center and its two neighbors to the left and right. The cell underneath shows the state of the center cell on the next row. As we proceed through the pattern on the first line, we apply each rule as determined by the pattern shown.

To get a better sense of how these rules work, use the following rules to fill out the grids below working from left to right, starting with the initial state given. Each grid has been started for you.

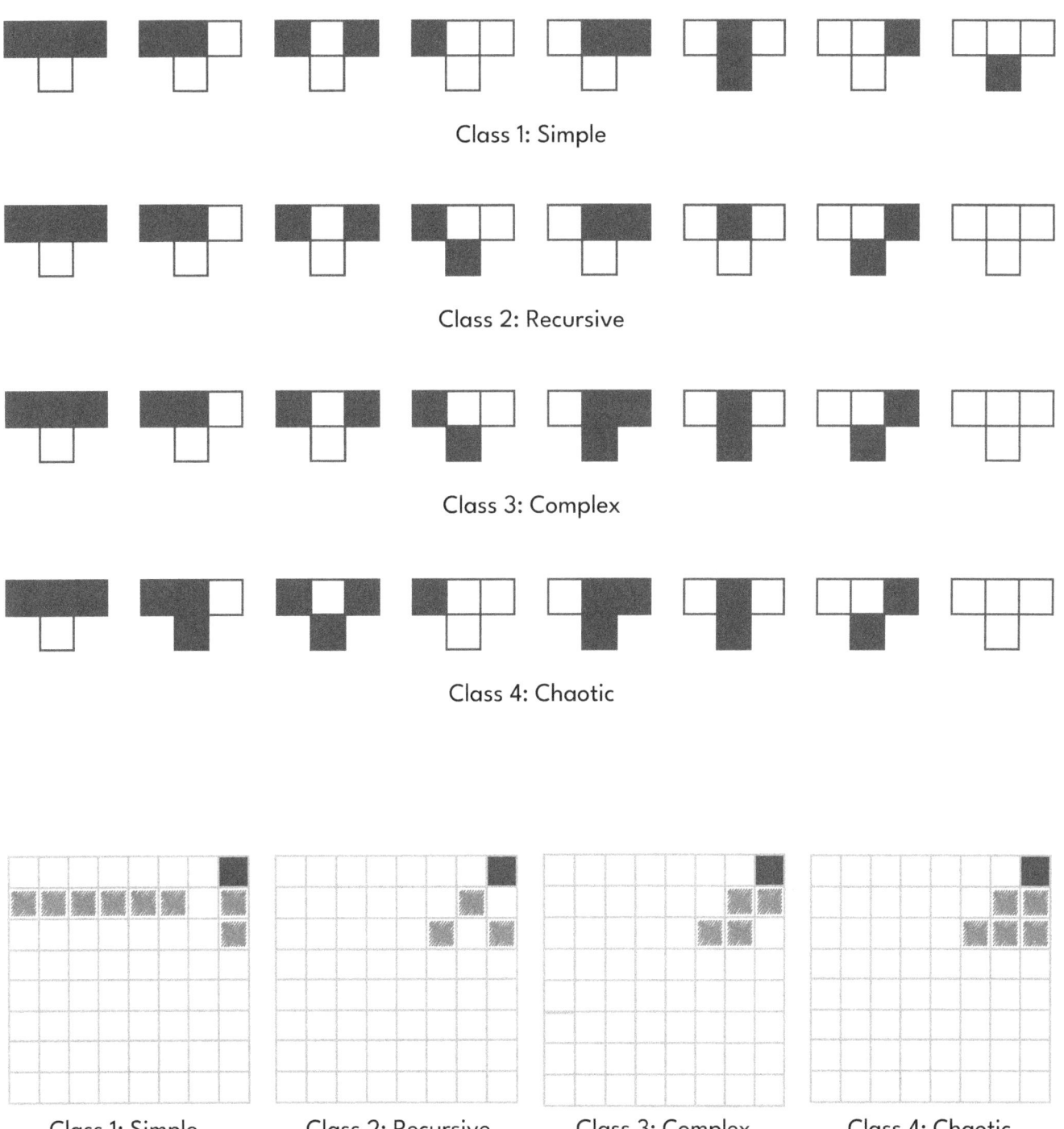

Class 1: Simple

Class 2: Recursive

Class 3: Complex

Class 4: Chaotic

Class 1: Simple   Class 2: Recursive   Class 3: Complex   Class 4: Chaotic

We Need a Hero

Let's apply this to a system that allows us to engineer complex behavior. This type of system is characterized by a little guy called a hero. ☺ The hero has a mood, indicated by his facial expression (☺ or ☹), and a direction, indicated by his sword (< or >). He travels back and forth in a one-dimensional dungeon, encountering items. Items may change his mood, his direction, or even cause him to move or change the item itself. But only the hero and his surroundings change from one timestep to the next. Everything else remains the same.

Here's an example rule for our hero, which causes him to move to the right when there's enough space for him to do so.

If we add a few more, we can make our hero do something. Here is a set of rules, and a dungeon, that makes the hero travel back and forth.

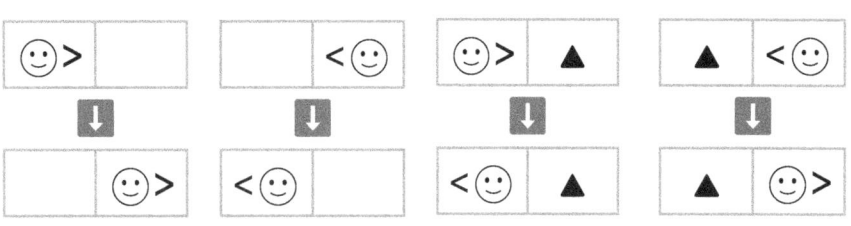

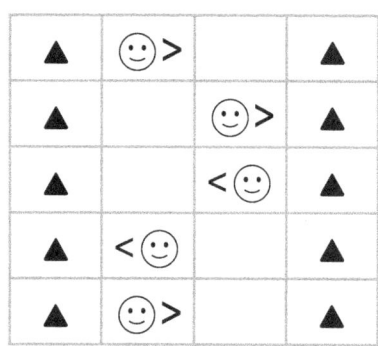

Our hero is capable of some pretty impressive stuff. For example, he can add 1 to any binary number with just a few rules and the right setup. Note: All cells on a row carry over to the row below, unless overwritten by our hero.

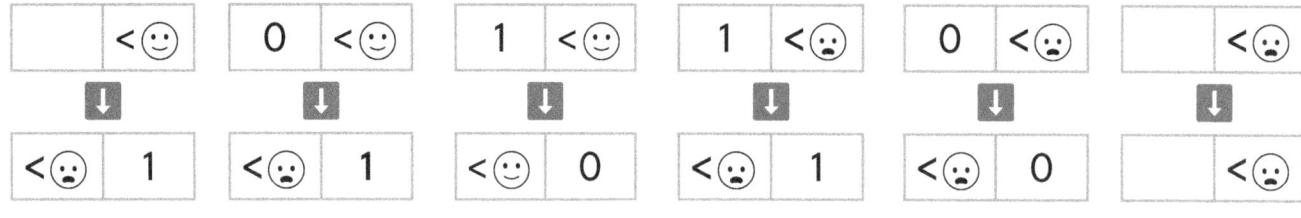

		1	1	1	<☺
		1	1	<☺	0
		1	<☺	0	0
		<☺	0	0	0
	<☹	1	0	0	0

The starting number, 111 in binary, is 7 in decimal. The final number, 1000 in binary, is 8 in decimal. Notice that the final rule, where the starting and ending states are identical, indicates a halting condition.

YOUR TURN:

You can see how finding the right rule to apply is a matter of looking at the hero and the cell the hero is pointed at. Our hero can do some fancier tricks. Try to apply the following rules to the dungeon. The first few lines have been filled out for you.

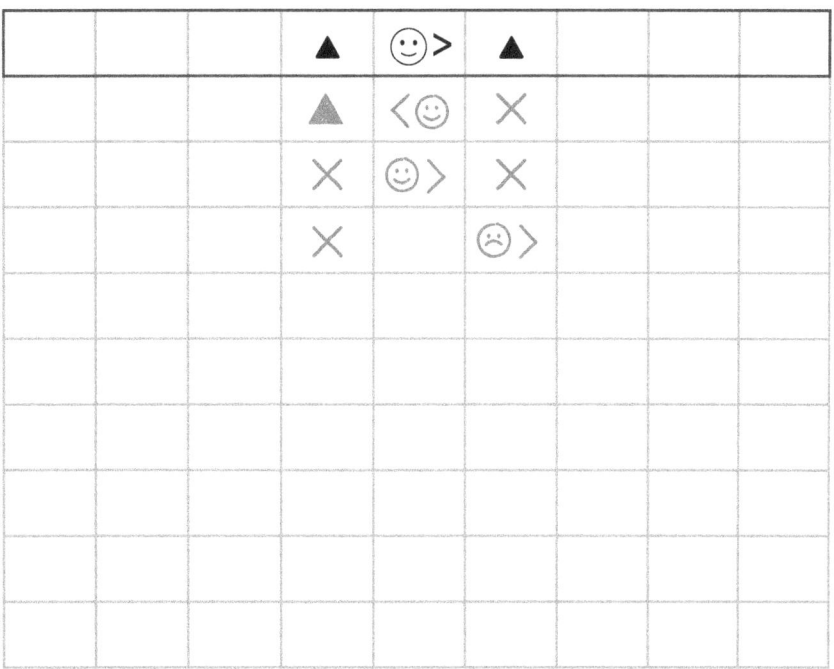

Taking It Further

Just to make sure you understand how our little guy works, combine the rules for adding 1 with the rules for moving back and forth in order to make a counter. The counter should keep adding 1 until it runs out of room and halts. Use as many additional moods for our hero and items in the dungeon as you need.

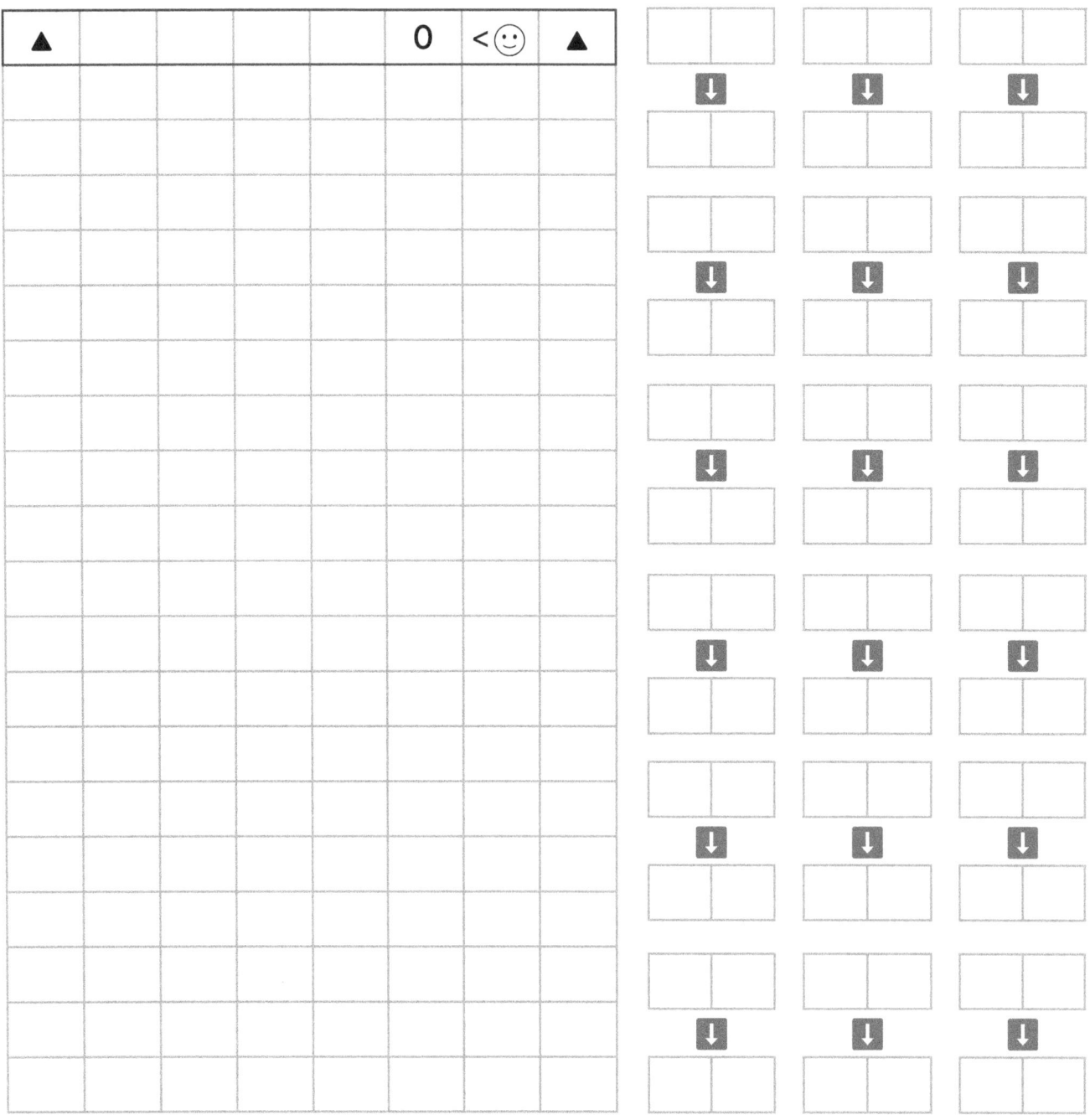

Your last task is to have fun. Treat the hero/dungeon system as a zero-player game and see what you can make it do. If you really want to challenge yourself, try to get your hero to exhibit class 3 (chaotic) behavior.

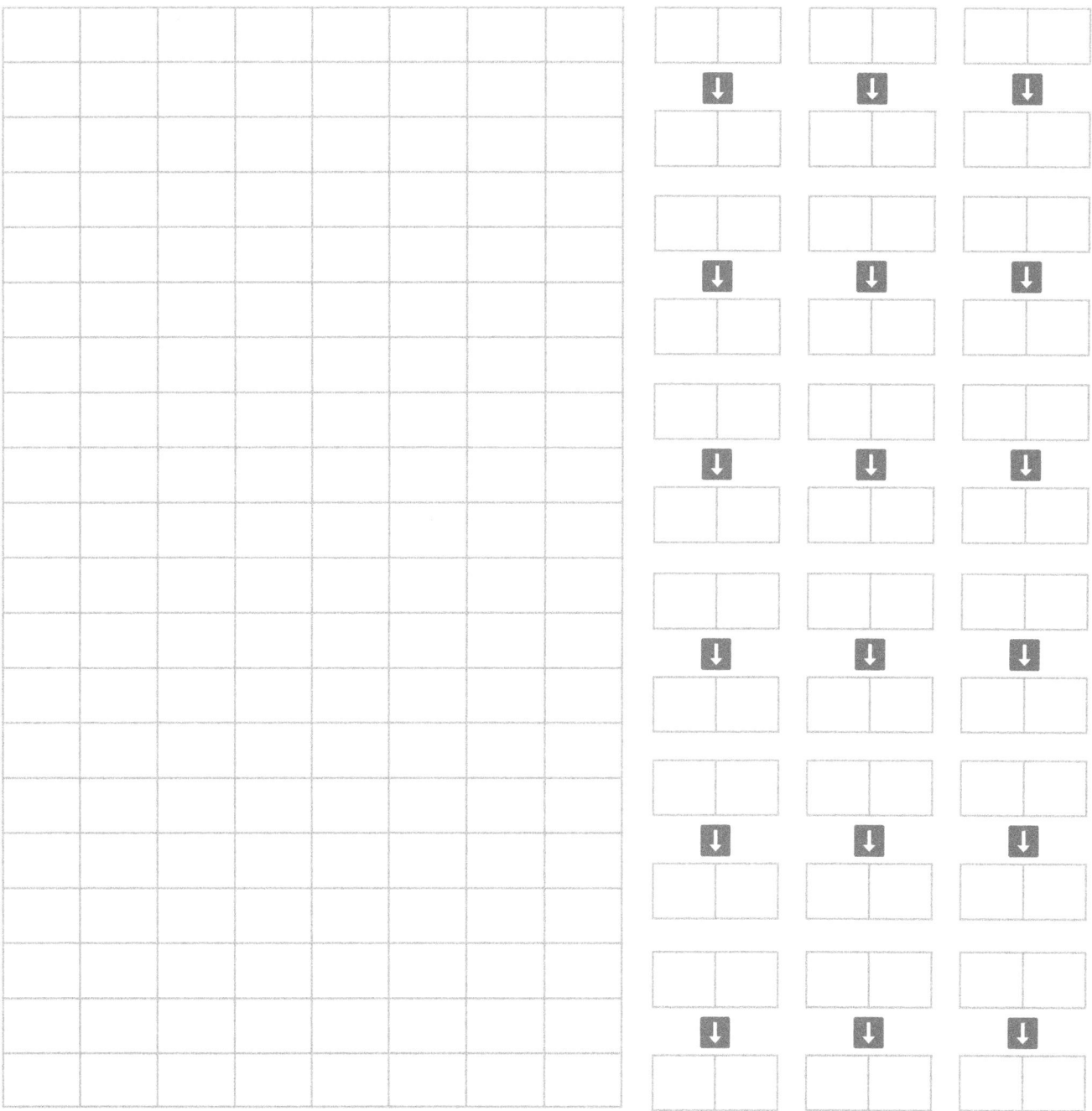

Guess what? Your hero is actually equivalent to a class of systems called "Turing machines," which were the first mathematical model that led to digital computing. They are still used as the benchmark of computational power today. We say anything that is capable of arbitrary transformations of information (e.g., a computer) is "Turing complete."

Breaking It Down: Balance

Balance, in the context of game design, is the term for making a game feel fair. Depending on the game, this may entail making it truly as fair as possible, or it may mean changing the players' perception.

The first and most rudimentary strategy in our balancing toolbox is symmetry. If all players (or all NPCs, etc.) have the same resources and actions available, the game is obviously fair. Games like chess and soccer/football fall into this category. In chess, the small advantage of moving first is neutralized by playing two games and switching sides in between. Similarly, any asymmetry caused by differences in the two halves of the soccer/football pitch are ironed out at half time when the two teams switch sides.

The second strategy is called "intransitivity." This refers to a situation where strategy A beats strategy B, and strategy B beats strategy C, but strategy A actually loses to strategy C. The most famous example, and one that's often used as a shorthand for intransitivity in general, is rock, paper, scissors (Roshambo). Any odd number of elements can have first-order intransitivity, like in the extended game Rock, Paper, Scissors, Lizard, Spock by Sam Kass and Karen Bryla.

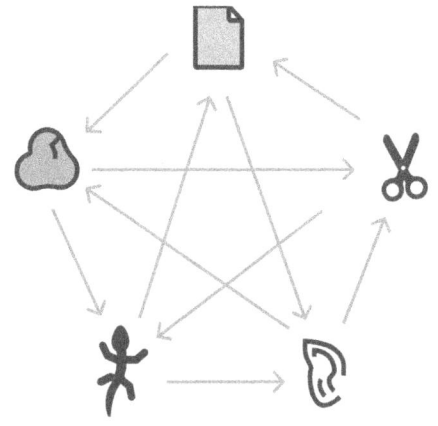

Intransitivity can also be achieved by breaking game elements down into numeric attributes and setting those attributes to asymmetric but overall balanced values. This can be done with individual elements but is usually done with strategies based on combinations of game elements that work well together, which are known as "synergies."

On the following page you'll see the classic RPG party. You can see how each contributes to a synergy. You could conceivably send a Fighter or Tank into battle alone, but their effectiveness goes up a lot if they have teammates. You'll notice that each archetype has one attribute at a high level, one at a medium level, and two at low levels, though no two archetypes have the same values for their attributes. This contributes to making them feel balanced.

The Classic RPG Party

	Fighter	Tank	Rogue	Healer	Ranger

Attack Damage	High	Med	Med	Negative Med	Med
Max Health	Med	High	Low	Low	Low
Speed	Low	Low	High	Low	Low
Range	Low	Low	Low	High	High

Your Task:

A game is described here, with the values of certain attributes missing. Read the game description and fill in the attributes as best you can.

A simultaneous turn-based strategy card game is being developed, with three card types as shown to the right.

  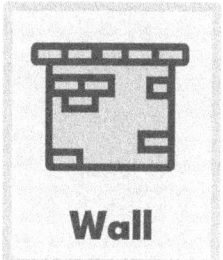

Tank　　　**Mine**　　　**Wall**

Each player begins with one mine, which produces some gold every turn. Players use gold to buy cards. Each player's goal is to destroy all of their opponent's cards. With two players there are three areas.

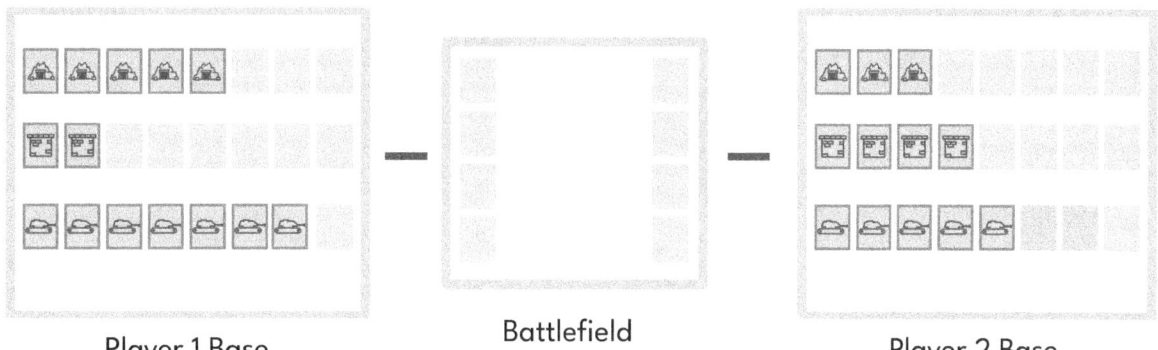

Player 1 Base　　　Battlefield　　　Player 2 Base

Newly purchased cards must be placed face down in the player's base with mines at the top, walls in the middle, and tanks at the bottom. Next, all tanks are moved from the base to the battlefield, where opposing tanks are annihilated in pairs. Any surviving tanks are moved to the enemy's base, where they attempt to destroy enemy cards, starting with walls. Walls can repel a certain number of tanks, but once that number reaches the threshold, the wall and all enemy tanks in its base are destroyed.

Four early-game strategies present themselves:

- Offensive - focus on tanks
- Defensive - focus on walls
- Production - focus on mines
- Mixed - a roughly even contribution from all unit types

Ideally, in a well-balanced game, all four of these strategies should be viable, though some may be weaker or stronger against others. No one strategy should dominate all others.

TIME TO GIVE IT A SHOT!

Try to set the following parameters to balance this game:

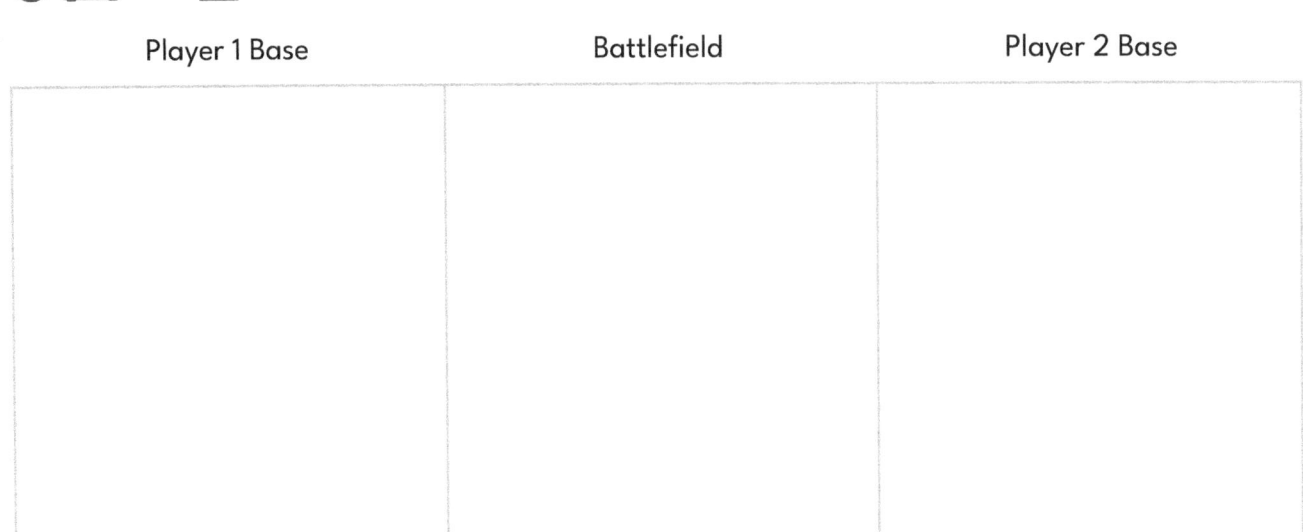

You may notice some mathematical relationships that seem to increase the odds that your chosen parameters are fair, but the only way to be sure is to test it. Use the following areas to play out several of these strategies against yourself to test the balance.

Player 1 Base	Battlefield	Player 2 Base

What a Concept: Randomness

It's now long-accepted wisdom in game design circles that randomness is a double-edged sword. It adds an approachability to games, making it possible for a newcomer to do much better, with a bit of luck, than they could have done with skill alone. Randomness, when implemented well, can keep games close and exciting even between competitors of very different proficiencies. It also takes from the player a measure of pride in accomplishment. Did they earn better results by making shrewd choices, or did they just get lucky this time? Also, a random loss of attained progress always feels severely discouraging.

There are a number of ways to incorporate randomness into a game, but broadly they fall into two categories.

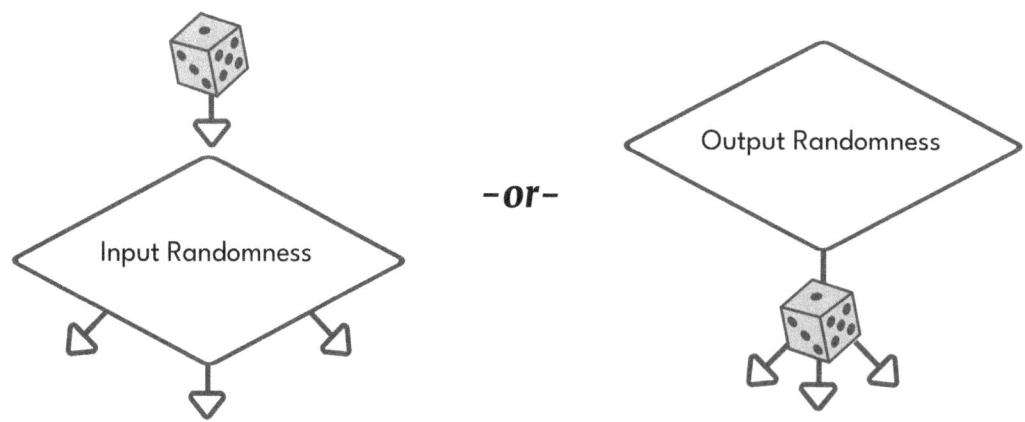

Input randomness is when random information is revealed to the player before they make a decision. For example, you see what hand you've been dealt in a game of poker before you decide what to wager.

Output randomness is when, after the player makes a decision, their degree of success depends upon a random factor, for example, hit-percentages in a turn-based tactical game like EXCOM, or rolling damage in a game like Dungeons & Dragons.

Each of these types of randomness has a very different flavor. Input randomness keeps the player alert—constantly reacting to a situation outside their control. Output randomness gives a game a looser, almost comedic, feeling. It encourages players to respond playfully to challenges and not take themselves too seriously.

Your mission is to write out your plan for how you would add randomness to a deterministic game that you are familiar with. In your new version of the game, something will be determined by the roll of one or more six-sided dice. Use the random dice rolls in the margins to test your idea.

Here are a few non-random games you could try:

- Chess
- Checkers
- Draughts
- Any Sport
- Go
- Reversi (Othello)
- Mancala
- Battleship
- Tic-Tac-Toe
- Stratego (L'Attaque)
- Diplomacy
- Connect Four

TRY IT:

What game will you be adding randomness to? Describe your new version of the game. Use diagrams to add clarity.

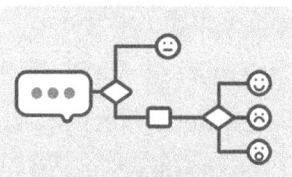

Narrative Design: Variables

This is an extension of the narrative design exercise "Story Flow" in Chapter 3. If you haven't done that exercise yet, consider doing that one first.

When we created an interactive story before, we used these four shapes:

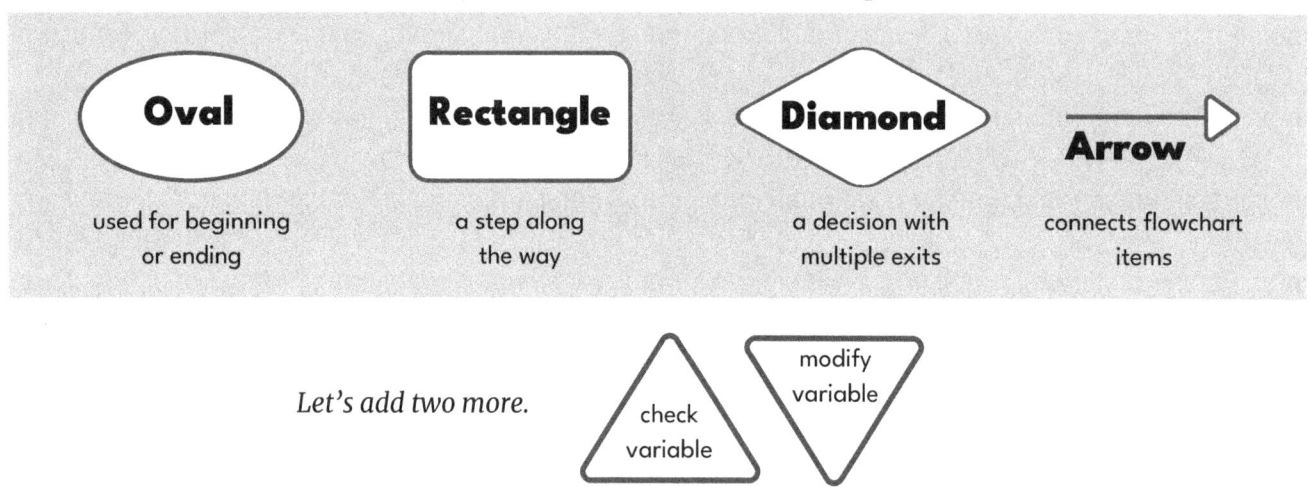

Oval	**Rectangle**	**Diamond**	**Arrow**
used for beginning or ending	a step along the way	a decision with multiple exits	connects flowchart items

Let's add two more.

check variable

modify variable

A variable is just a name that we associate with a remembered value. For instance, we might use a variable to keep track of how much money a main character has.

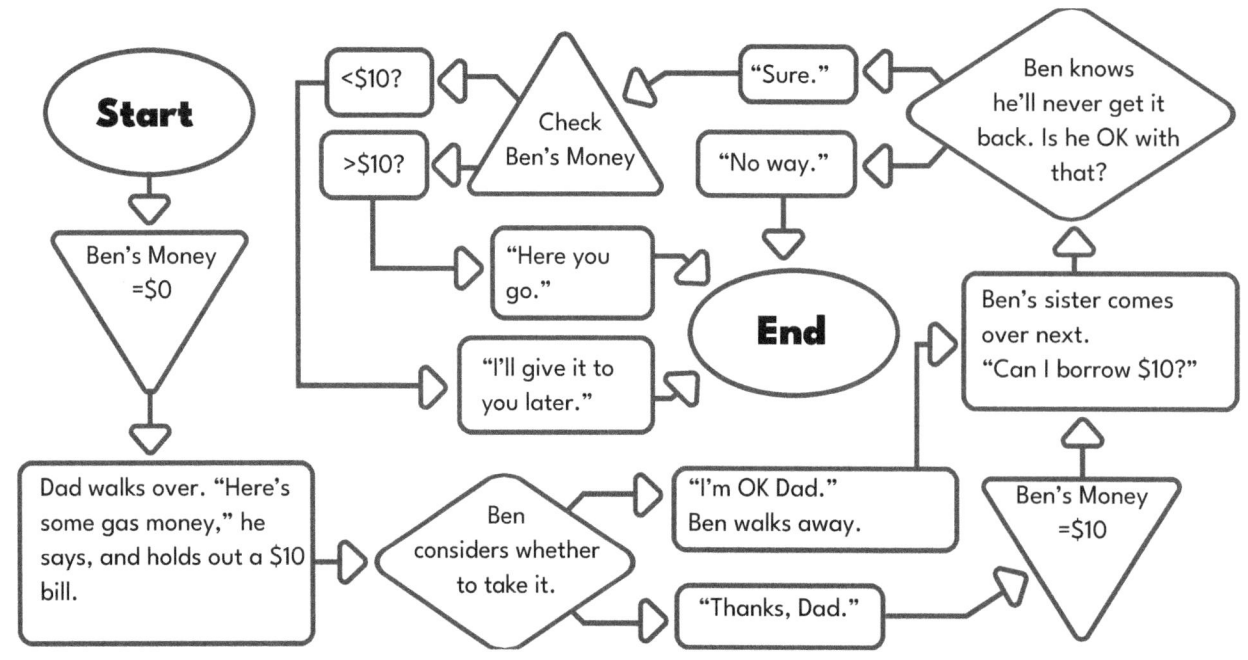

Your Turn

Create another simple story below that keeps track of at least one variable, or "stat." The variable might be how happy someone feels on a scale of 1 to 10, or percent blood alcohol level, or how many sheep are in a herd. For this exercise, try to stay away from traditional game stats like health, ammo, charisma, etc.

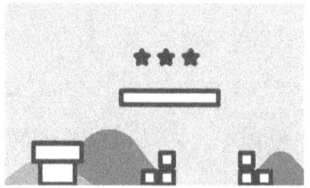

Level Design: Race Track

Race track is a pen-and-paper game where two or more players compete in a race. Each player starts along a starting line, and they take turns moving through the track without colliding with the walls. First to the finish line wins!

To move, players start by moving to one of the eight neighboring grid points around their starting position. Every subsequent move must be either to the spot they would arrive at if they went the same speed and direction as last turn *or* to one of the eight neighboring points around that spot.

For Example:

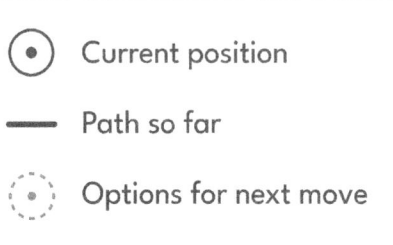

Start

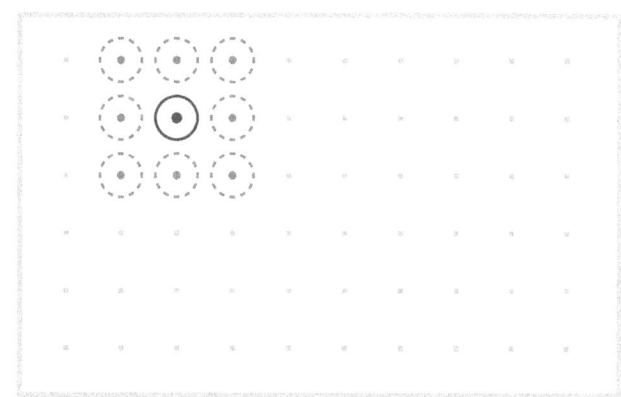

1st Move

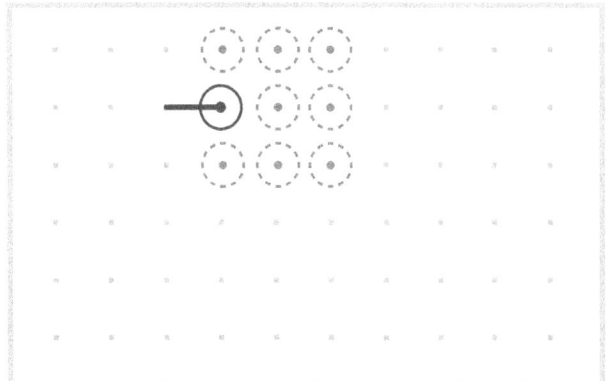

2nd Move

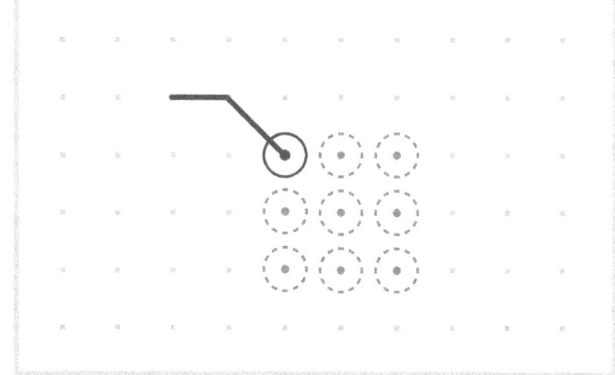

Play a round against yourself to get a feel for the game. Count the number of moves it took to get around the course as each player.

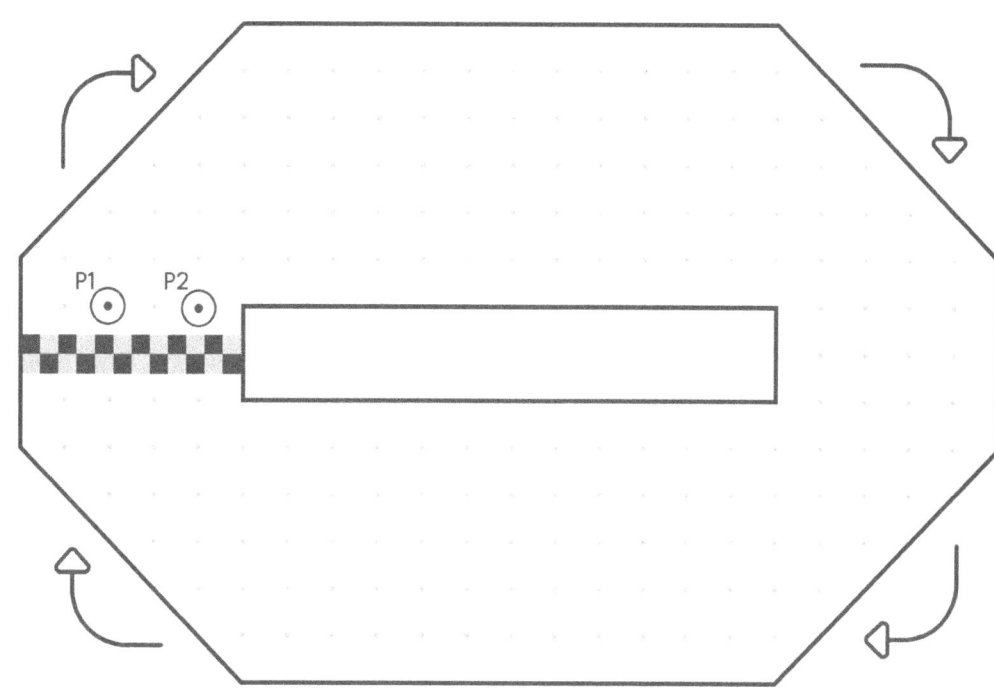

YOUR TURN:

In the following space and next page, design some new tracks. Try to make them as fair as possible by counting the minimum distance each player would need to travel to complete the course. Give each track a reason for existing. In other words, ask yourself, "What is interesting about this particular track?"

For the next track you design, think about adding some completely new elements. Obstacles? Teleporters? Really go wild.

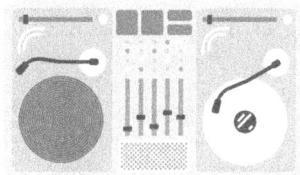

Remix: Battling Ships

The Rules of Battling Ships:

1 🔒 Play takes place on two 10x10 grids, one for each player.

2 Each player chooses where to place their "ships," which occupy rectangular grid spaces 1x2, 1x2, 1x3, 1x4, and 1x5. These can be turned 90° as well, so they can be aligned horizontally and vertically.

3 Players take turns announcing the coordinates of a single space to fire at.

4 When one player fires, the other player must say truthfully whether it was a "hit" (i.e., that space is occupied by part of a ship) or a "miss."

5 If every space occupied by a ship has been hit, that ship is "sunk."

6 When all of one player's ships have been sunk, the other player has won.

Mountain Fold

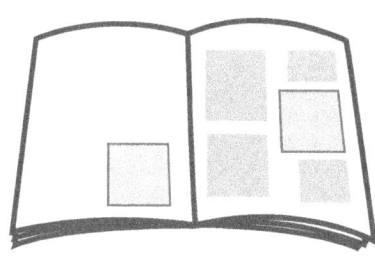

To play with a friend:

Begin by playing a round of the standard game. If you can find someone to play with, fold over page 151 and use it as a barrier between the two players' play areas.

To play on your own:

If you're playing alone, don't fold over the page; it supplies an NPC to play against, so rotate the book and play using the topmost of the two grids on the next page, following the instructions on the NPC opponent page to play.

TIME TO PLAY!

Play a game either against the NPC or a friend and then return here and revisit some rules of the game. What would you change? Did the game feel balanced? Well-paced? What kinds of mechanics could you add to make the game more interesting, challenging, or exciting? Use the spaces below to design new rules

Opponent's grid:

Ignore this if playing the NPC.

	1	2	3	4	5	6	7	8	9	10
A										
B										
C										
D										
E										
F										
G										
H										
I										
J										

Your grid:

Use this grid to place your ships. You'll place five ships of the lengths shown on the left across the board.

	1	2	3	4	5	6	7	8	9	10
A										
B										
C										
D										
E										
F										
G										
H										
I										
J										

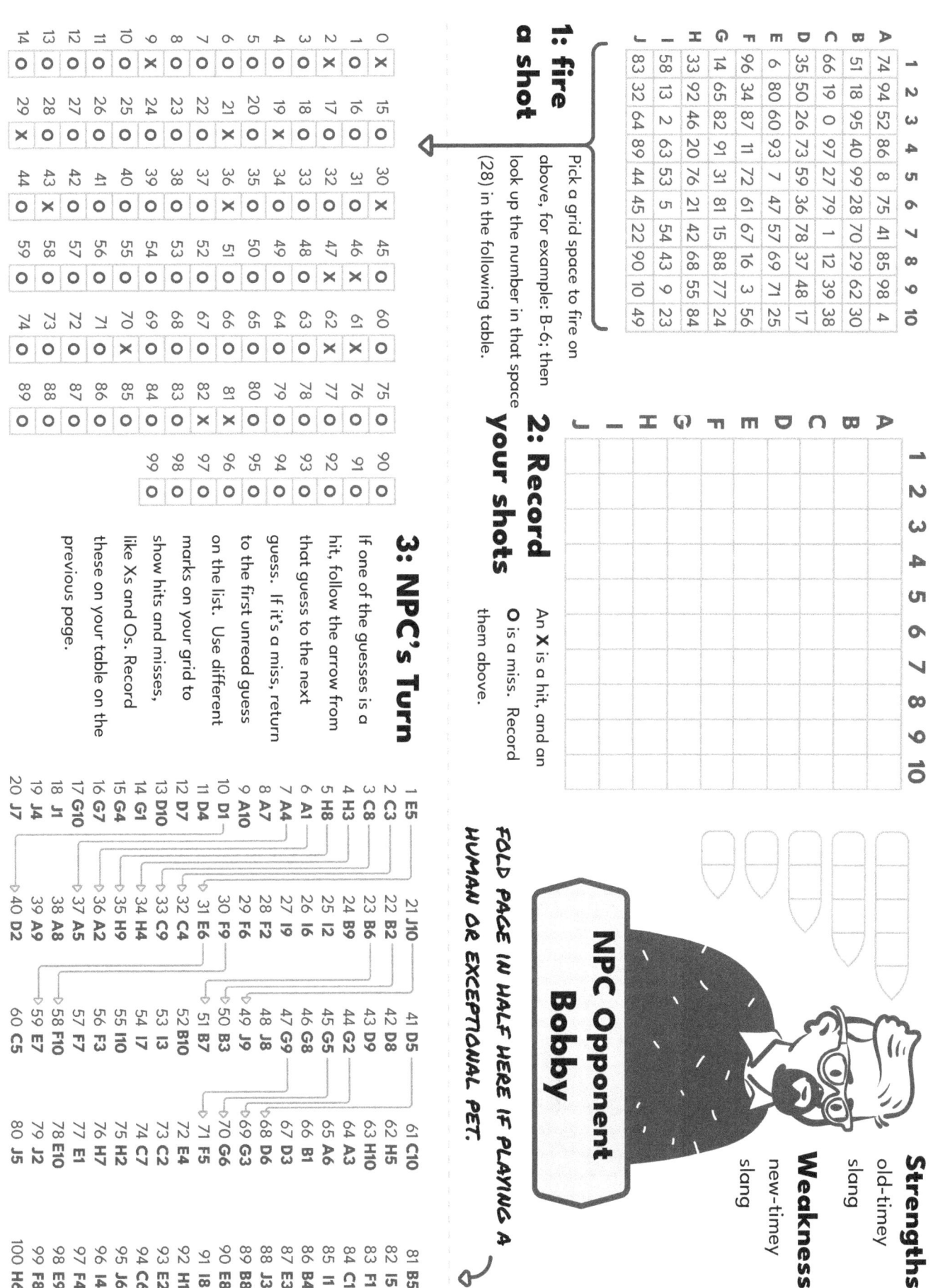

Strengths:
old-timey slang

Weakness:
new-timey slang

NPC Opponent Bobby

FOLD PAGE IN HALF HERE IF PLAYING A HUMAN OR EXCEPTIONAL PET.

1: fire a shot

Pick a grid space to fire on above, for example: B-6; then look up the number in that space (28) in the following table.

	1	2	3	4	5	6	7	8	9	10
A	74	94	52	86	8	75	41	85	98	4
B	51	18	95	40	99	28	70	29	62	30
C	66	19	0	97	27	79	1	12	39	38
D	35	50	26	73	59	36	78	37	48	17
E	6	80	60	93	7	47	57	69	71	25
F	96	34	87	11	72	61	67	16	3	56
G	14	65	82	91	31	81	15	88	77	24
H	33	92	46	20	76	21	42	68	55	84
I	58	13	2	63	53	5	54	43	9	23
J	83	32	64	89	44	45	22	90	10	49

0 X	15 X	30 X	45 O	60 O	75 O	90 O
1 O	16 O	31 O	46 X	61 X	76 O	91 O
2 X	17 O	32 O	47 X	62 X	77 O	92 O
3 O	18 O	33 O	48 O	63 O	78 O	93 O
4 O	19 X	34 O	49 O	64 O	79 O	94 O
5 O	20 O	35 O	50 O	65 O	80 O	95 O
6 O	21 X	36 X	51 O	66 O	81 X	96 O
7 O	22 O	37 O	52 O	67 O	82 X	97 O
8 O	23 O	38 O	53 O	68 O	83 O	98 O
9 X	24 O	39 O	54 O	69 O	84 O	99 O
10 O	25 O	40 O	55 O	70 X	85 O	
11 O	26 O	41 O	56 O	71 O	86 O	
12 O	27 O	42 O	57 O	72 O	87 O	
13 O	28 O	43 X	58 O	73 O	88 O	
14 O	29 X	44 O	59 O	74 O	89 O	

2: Record your shots

An **X** is a hit, and an **O** is a miss. Record them above.

	1	2	3	4	5	6	7	8	9	10
A										
B										
C										
D										
E										
F										
G										
H										
I										
J										

3: NPC's Turn

If one of the guesses is a hit, follow the arrow from that guess to the next guess. If it's a miss, return to the first unread guess on the list. Use different marks on your grid to show hits and misses, like Xs and Os. Record these on your table on the previous page.

1 E5	21 J10	41 D5	61 C10	81 B5
2 C3	22 B2	42 D8	62 H5	82 I5
3 C8	23 B6	43 D9	63 H10	83 F1
4 H3	24 B9	44 G2	64 A3	84 C1
5 H8	25 I2	45 G5	65 A6	85 I1
6 A1	26 I6	46 G8	66 B1	86 B4
7 A4	27 I9	47 G9	67 D3	87 E3
8 A7	28 F2	48 J8	68 D6	88 J3
9 A10	29 F6	49 J9	69 G3	89 B8
10 D1	30 F9	50 B3	70 G6	90 E8
11 D4	31 E6	51 B7	71 F5	91 I8
12 D7	32 C4	52 B10	72 E4	92 H1
13 D10	33 C9	53 I3	73 C2	93 E2
14 G1	34 H4	54 I7	74 C7	94 C6
15 G4	35 H9	55 I10	75 H2	95 J6
16 G7	36 A2	56 F3	76 H7	96 I4
17 G10	37 A5	57 F7	77 E1	97 F4
18 J1	38 A8	58 F10	78 E10	98 E9
19 J4	39 A9	59 E7	79 J2	99 F8
20 J7	40 D2	60 C5	80 J5	100 H6

Strengths: powerful dad-sneeze

Weakness: powerful dad-sneeze

NPC Opponent Eric

FOLD PAGE IN HALF HERE IF PLAYING A HUMAN OR EXCEPTIONAL PET.

1: fire a shot

Pick a grid space to fire on above, for example: B-6; then look up the number in that space (16) in the following table.

	1	2	3	4	5	6	7	8	9	10
A	10	92	55	99	21	96	4	56	11	76
B	83	59	30	60	98	16	65	84	39	23
C	29	74	1	17	54	91	38	3	90	46
D	58	97	45	72	24	31	64	22	57	73
E	47	9	77	37	78	6	7	27	66	18
F	82	28	93	12	32	69	40	33	85	49
G	19	63	48	81	51	25	95	15	94	70
H	36	75	52	2	20	67	26	80	8	86
I	53	5	35	62	41	13	87	0	34	50
J	68	88	42	43	79	14	71	44	89	61

2: Record your shots

An **X** is a hit, and an **O** is a miss. record them above.

3: NPC's Turn

If one of the guesses is a hit, follow the arrow from that guess to the next guess. If it's a miss, return to the first unread guess on the list. Use different marks on your grid to show hits and misses, like Xs and Os. Record these on your table on the previous page.

NPC guess list

#	Cell	#	Cell	#	Cell	#	Cell	#	Cell
1	A1	21	A2	41	A3	61	A4	81	A5
2	B2	22	B3	42	B4	62	B5	82	B1
3	C3	23	C4	43	C5	63	C6	83	C7
4	D4	24	D5	44	D6	64	D1	84	D2
5	E5	25	E4	45	E3	65	E2	85	E1
6	F6	26	F7	46	F8	66	F9	86	F10
7	G7	27	G8	47	G9	67	G10	87	G3
8	H8	28	H9	48	H10	68	H1	88	H2
9	I9	29	I10	49	I7	69	I8	89	I1
10	J10	30	J9	50	J8	70	J7	90	J6
11	J1	31	J2	51	J3	71	J4	91	J5
12	I2	32	I3	52	I4	72	I5	92	I6
13	H3	33	H4	53	H5	73	H6	93	H7
14	G4	34	G5	54	G6	74	G1	94	G2
15	F5	35	F4	55	F3	75	F2	95	F1
16	E6	36	E7	56	E8	76	E9	96	E10
17	D7	37	D8	57	D9	77	D10	97	D3
18	C8	38	C9	58	C10	78	C1	98	C2
19	B9	39	B10	59	B6	79	B7	99	B8
20	A10	40	A9	60	A8	80	A7	100	A6

Shot record table

#	Mark	#	Mark	#	Mark	#	Mark	#	Mark	#	Mark	#	Mark
0	O	15	X	30	O	45	O	60	O	75	O	90	X
1	O	16	O	31	O	46	O	61	X	76	O	91	X
2	O	17	O	32	O	47	O	62	O	77	O	92	O
3	X	18	O	33	X	48	X	63	O	78	O	93	X
4	O	19	O	34	O	49	O	64	O	79	O	94	O
5	O	20	O	35	X	50	O	65	O	80	O	95	O
6	O	21	O	36	O	51	O	66	O	81	O	96	O
7	O	22	O	37	O	52	X	67	O	82	O	97	O
8	O	23	O	38	X	53	O	68	O	83	X	98	O
9	O	24	O	39	O	54	X	69	O	84	O	99	O
10	O	25	O	40	O	55	O	70	O	85	O		
11	O	26	O	41	O	56	O	71	O	86	O		
12	X	27	X	42	O	57	O	72	O	87	O		
13	O	28	O	43	O	58	O	73	O	88	O		
14	O	29	O	44	O	59	X	74	O	89	X		

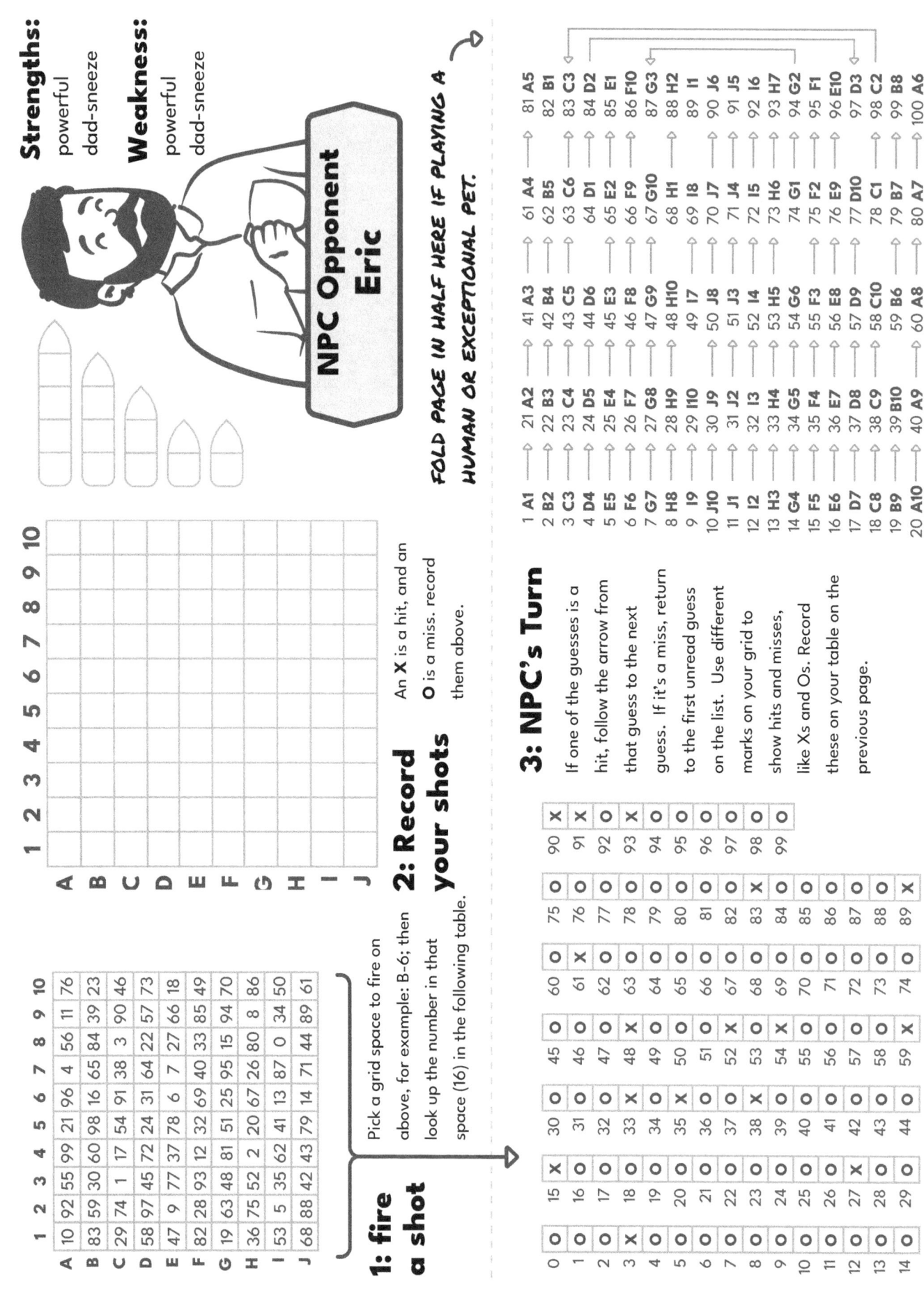

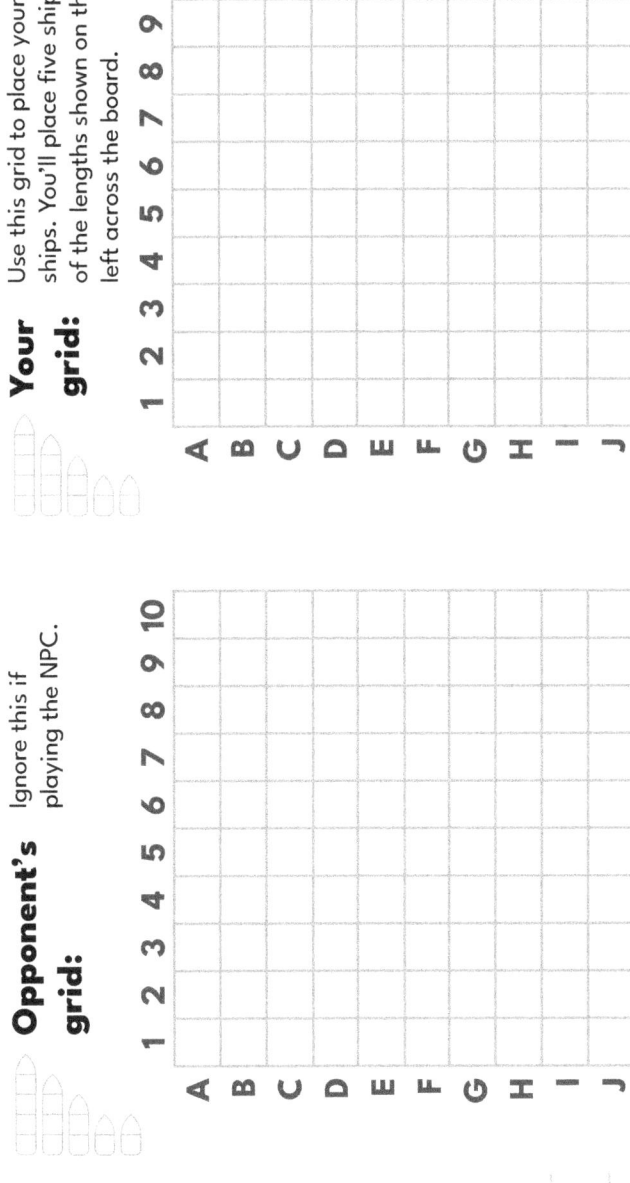

Opponent's grid: Ignore this if playing the NPC.

	1	2	3	4	5	6	7	8	9	10
A										
B										
C										
D										
E										
F										
G										
H										
I										
J										

Your grid: Use this grid to place your ships. You'll place five ships of the lengths shown on the left across the board.

	1	2	3	4	5	6	7	8	9	10
A										
B										
C										
D										
E										
F										
G										
H										
I										
J										

TIME TO PLAY!

Play a game either against the NPC or a friend and then return here and revisit some rules of the game. What would you change? Did the game feel balanced? Well-paced? What kinds of mechanics could you add to make the game more interesting, challenging, or exciting?

Use the spaces below to design new rules

What a Concept: Randomness 2

This time, it's entropic.

The amount of randomness in games can vary wildly, and every game falls along a spectrum.

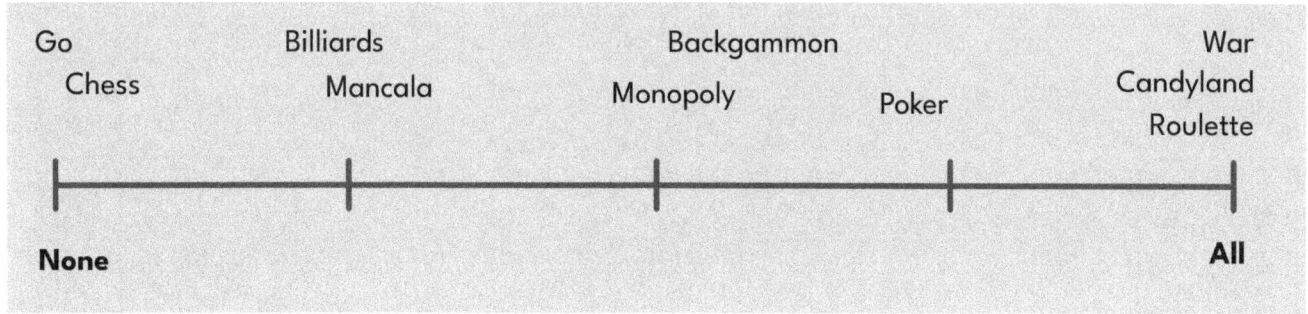

In the previous randomness exercise (Chapter 6, "What a Concept: Randomness"), you were tasked to choose a game from the left side of this spectrum and, with the addition of one or more elements, shove it closer to the middle. In this task, you must do the opposite—choose a game closer to the right side of the spectrum and find a way to remove as much randomness as you can, while maintaining the parts of the game that make it a unique and worthwhile play experience. Gambling games are good candidates, as are games of pure chance for young children.

Because adding randomness is a much simpler and more intuitive undertaking than removing it (second law of thermodynamics, anyone?), we've provided some tools on the next page for reducing randomness in a game system.

Shuffle and Deal: If you need to get to a state where each player has a hand of cards, rather than simply deal one card to each player in a circuit, deal two or three cards to each player in a round robin and force each player to discard all but one.

Repeated Dice Rolls: If players need to roll dice repeatedly, give them a fixed amount of each possible rolled result, and let them choose when to spend them.

Bid Against the House and Each Other: For games where hidden information is not an important component, give players a budget to spend on cards, dice rolls, or whatever resource is important for the game.

Replace Strict Hierarchies With Intransitivity: Intransitivity is the quality that games have when all strategies are balanced as in rock, paper, scissors. This doesn't reduce randomness directly, but it should help you to reframe challenges in the game in terms of decision-making rather than luck. For instance, you could use intransitive dice.* Or you might say that in your poker variant a flush still beats a straight and a full house still beats a flush, but now a straight beats a full house. Now players need to concentrate on strategies to counter their opponents, rather than just acquire the strongest hand possible.

Old: Full House > Flush > Straight

New: Straight > Full House > Flush > Straight

Pre-Stack: Allow players to prearrange their own cards or dice or what-have-you in whatever order they'd like. When the time comes, players simultaneously reveal the choices they've made previously and then determine the results.

*Intransitive Dice

It is a non-intuitive fact that particular sets of dice exhibit intransitivity on average after repeated rolls. For example, take the set of cube-shaped dice shown to the right.

	4		
4	9	2	2
	9		

A

	1		
1	6	8	8
	6		

B

	3		
3	5	7	7
	5		

C

A > B
B > C
C > A

GIVE IT A SHOT

This is not a straightforward challenge, so we will provide you ample space here. Good luck...or should we say good choices?

Chapter Seven

Outside the Box

———

Let us think the unthinkable, let us do the undoable.
Let us prepare to grapple with the ineffable itself, and
see if we may not eff it after all.

—Douglas Adams

Reflection: Player Creativity

Players like to express themselves. When players exercise their imagination in a game, they have invested a piece of themselves in that game and are much less likely to leave it behind thoughtlessly. The most common outlets for player creativity are avatar customization and decorating virtual spaces. In both cases, the effect on gameplay is usually small to nonexistent. That places player creativity within the meaning-making frame of a game experience, but outside the core gameplay.

Players may also be confronted with open-ended puzzles, which allow the player to craft unique and creative solutions. The game can still assess whether a victory condition has been met, but the player gets to feel that they left their mark. Unfortunately for developers, if the system is truly free enough for the player to feel creative within it, it is probably also very difficult to test and debug.

When one thinks of creativity, they think of art forms like painting, musical composition, or theater. These endeavors are impossible to assess in any automated way and are often controversial even among humans. Thus, the only way to include them is to make them self-assessed, which is to say remove them from any consequence or allow other players to weigh in. Party games, for instance, sometimes include drawing or acting, which other players must judge.

The downside of requiring a player to be creative is that many people are intimidated by an empty canvas. They may be too nervous to get started or too self-critical to be satisfied with their results.

Can you think of any other ways player creativity is used in games? What level of creative affordance do you prefer as a player? How would you like to allow for player creativity in your own practice as a game designer?

User-Generated Content

When player creativity can be shared in a digital multiplayer game, it's often called "user-generated content (UGC)." Game studios have a big incentive to enable users to create and share, as every minute users interact with UGC is one less minute that needs to be created by the studio. The spirit of UGC within a particular game can range from empowering to exploitative. Consider that dichotomy as you write your thoughts.

Cross-Training: Theme Park Design

In some ways, theme parks are what games, especially videogames, wish they could be: immersive, visceral, immediate, and embodied. In other ways, they lack the things that make games worthwhile: meaningful decision-making, long-term progress, and the pride of accomplishment (or the shame of defeat). Still, there is much that game designers have learned from their older cousins in themed entertainment and much we have yet to learn.

In this exercise you'll be designing a theme park of your own, starting with the high-level concept. As we discussed in the exercise "Narrative Design: Theming," a theme really consists of two parts: the dramatic theme and the manifestation theme. If someone asked what the *Fast and the Furious* movie franchise is about, you could answer "cool cars"; that's the manifestation theme. Or you could answer "family and loyalty"; that's the dramatic theme.

Let's start with the manifestation theme. They say there are three things that draw an audience to a themed experience: the Head, the Heart, and the Stomach.

The Head: Something the guest is intellectually interested in
The Heart: Something the guest aspires to do
The Stomach: Something that creates a pleasant visceral experience

Picking a Manifestation Theme:

For the purposes of this exercise, you can't use privately owned intellectual property, but I've included a list of fun public domain properties you can use, if you choose.

My Manifestation Theme:

- Alice in Wonderland
- The Wizard of Oz
- Peter Pan
- Doctor Doolittle
- The works of H.G. Wells
- Tarzan
- Winnie the Pooh
- Frankenstein
- Sherlock Holmes
- Paul Bunyan
- King Arthur
- Greek Mythology (Hercules)
- West African Mythology (Anansi)
- The Works of Shakespeare
- The Odyssey

The next thing to determine is the dramatic theme of your park. Dramatic themes are usually terse messages about life, such as "You can do anything you set your mind to" or "Power corrupts." Think about the point of view your manifestation theme represents. For instance, if your manifestation theme were "military pilots of World War I," a reasonable dramatic theme could be "You must fight for what you believe in." Try to keep your dramatic theme short and sweet.

My Dramatic Theme:

Now imagine you're a new visitor to your theme park. You've just paid for entry and gone through the turnstiles. Just over the hill is the entrance gate, and the name of the park is written across it in an appropriate typeface.

My Park Name:

Soon you'll be asked to draw a map of your theme park, but first let's analyze some anonymized maps of existing theme parks.

Notice how the park layout guides attendees toward the central sculpture, lured by the weenie just beyond it. From there the pathways branch out in a pattern known as "hub and spoke." This increases the park's capacity (and reduces queues) by spreading attendees evenly across attractions. It also keeps guests from getting lost.

Key

- Interesting Boundaries
- Berm
- Attraction
- Transportation
- ▲ Weenie
- Sculpture
- "Land" Boundary
- Water
- Foliage

Berm: An earthworks wall that serves to block sightlines while masquerading as a natural feature.

Weenie: An attraction or sculpture that can be seen from far away and used to navigate.

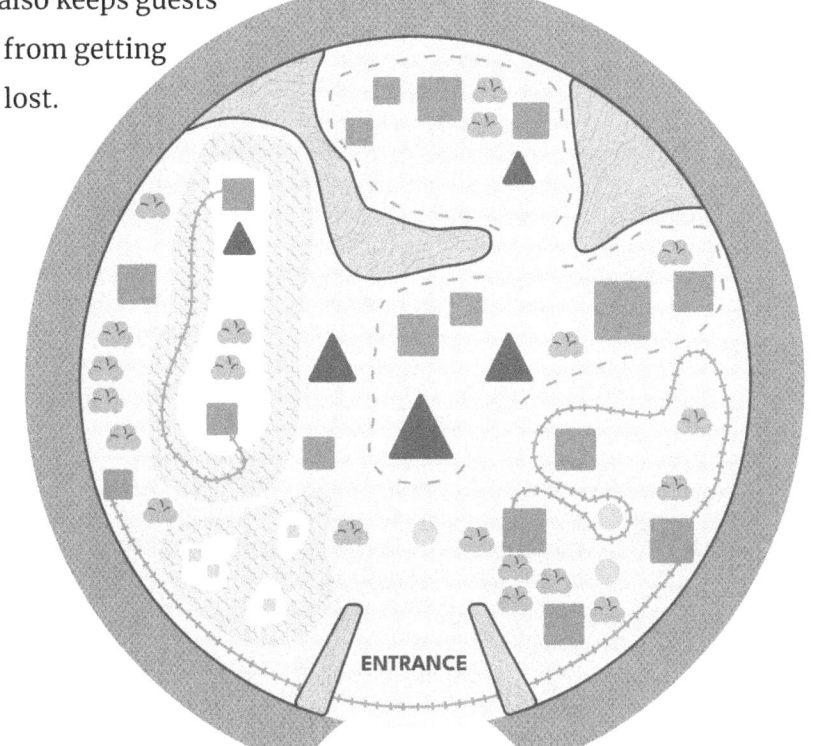

ENTRANCE

Let's look in greater detail at a partial map of another park.

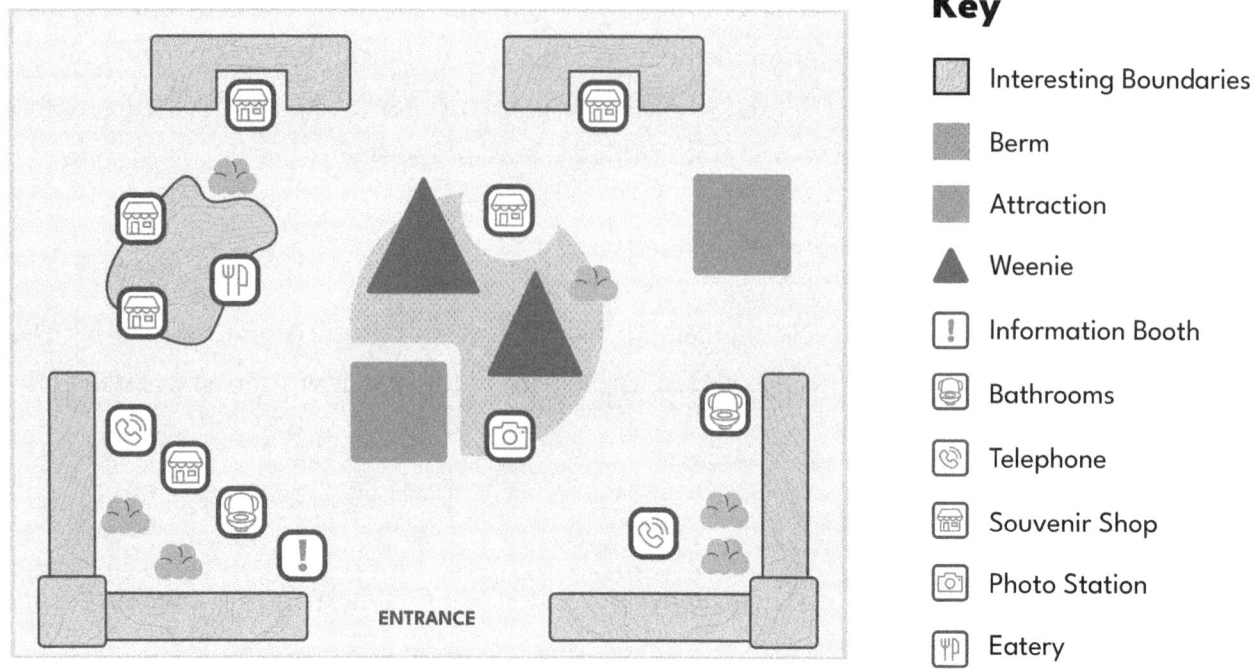

Key

◻ Interesting Boundaries

▦ Berm

▦ Attraction

▲ Weenie

! Information Booth

Bathrooms

☏ Telephone

Souvenir Shop

Photo Station

Eatery

You can see how each attraction is supported by lots of ancillary facilities—gift shops, restrooms, eateries, etc. It's also possible for a souvenir shop to be an attraction.

YOUR TURN!

Draw a map of the theme park you brainstormed earlier in this exercise. Make it about the size of one of the "lands" in the first example map. That's about two to three times the size of the second example map. There is more space on the following page.

Can you take it any further? A few ideas:

- An attraction that travels through berms, weenies, or shops
- An area of the park that is accessible only to certain visitors, or during certain times
- An attraction that changes during a time of the year, like a roller coaster that runs backward during Halloween

Breaking It Down: Bodies

To get a grasp on the design of a game, we must decompose the game and its subjects and themes. In this exercise, you'll try to break an activity undertaken with your body into pieces that can be better understood by the player and better manipulated by you, the designer. As an example of the sort of thing we're asking, take Ninja. Ninja is a playground game that effectively breaks down an epic hand-to-hand confrontation between two or more ninja into short turn-based steps.

The Rules of Ninja:

1. 2-10 players stand in a circle with their hands pressed together and pointed toward the center of the circle.

2. A chosen player counts down: "3, 2, 1, Ninja!"

3. When the chosen player says "ninja," all players move backward into a ninja pose and freeze.

4. Players take turns clockwise around the circle, starting with the chosen player.

5. The object of the game is to strike the other players (gently) in their limbs with a kick or karate chop. Limbs that have been struck become disabled. Disabled arms must be tucked behind the player's back. If a single leg is disabled, the player must stand on the other leg. If both legs are disabled, they must play on their knees.

6. The last player with one or more limbs remaining is the winner.

7. On a player's turn, they perform a single fluid motion with their body. The motion may include a single step. Usually, this motion is an attempted blow to another player's limb.

8. Players who are being attacked also may make a single fluid motion to attempt to avoid being hit.

9. When the turn is done, both attackers and defenders must freeze in place until the next turn.

In Ninja, movements are discretized by being able to take at most one step per turn, as well as the constraint of fluidity. Human bodies have natural endpoints to the movements of our joints, and continuing to move by changing the direction of motion would violate the fluidity. The body itself is also discretized into the four limbs.

In this exercise, your task is to create a similar turn-based game with no equipment, patterned after a physical activity, as Ninja is patterned after unarmed combat. We've listed a few activity ideas here. Feel free to use one of these or to discover your own.

- A Secret Handshake
- An Armwrestling Match
- A Foot Race
- Professional Wrestling

- Ballroom Dance
- Sneaking Past Guards
- Tag
- A Breakdance Battle

- Cheerleading
- A Training Montage

Whatever activity you choose to adapt, you should consider carefully how you will keep your players safe, and how they will establish and continue to signal their consent to take part in a game that will almost certainly involve physical touch or, at the least, intrusions into one another's personal space.

You'll write the rules of your new game on the following pages. If you need to specify zones of the body itself, mark them on the figure here, or in the case of hand-based games, on the hands:

OUTLINE YOUR TURN-BASED GAME IDEA HERE:

As you specify your game, you should also consider how you might adapt the rules for players with nonstandard bodies.

Narrative Design: Micro-RPG

The original tabletop role-playing games (TTRPGs), such as Dungeons & Dragons, often required multiple volumes to fully specify. Recently, there's been a trend of creating much simpler TTRPG systems that can be communicated in a few pages. The lack of detail is compensated for by keeping the playtimes short and by putting more faith in the players and the game-master, if any. The following is a basic example.

Miami Home for Retired Superheroes

- 1-6 players
- All Audiences
- 15m playtime

You and your friends are retired superheroes in the cafeteria of an assisted living facility. Each player should come up with their superhero name, their superpower, and how that superpower has degraded with old age.

Each player takes their turn rolling a six-sided dice, re-rolling any numbers previously rolled, and consulting the following table to tell a story about the good old days. They should talk about a time when...

1 A superhero comrade died

2 You saved someone else at the table

3 You had a falling out with a sidekick

4 You narrowly avoided death

5 You were given an award or honor

6 Your secret identity was revealed to someone

As others are telling their stories, players should feel free to heckle them, to chime in with details, to remember the same events differently, or to fill everyone in on what's become of the people mentioned. Once everyone has told their story...

OH NO! One of your old villains, Professor Nasty, bursts through the wall of the cafeteria in the Nastymobile, and he's looking for revenge. Go around the table and take turns narrating how you work together to take him down.

The End

Try playing Miami Home for Retired Superheroes either by yourself or with others. The goal of this style of TTRPG is not to solve problems or to win; it's to have fun and to tell an entertaining story. The designer has to balance giving players enough of a framework to make storytelling less intimidating, while also allowing enough freedom to play and fitting the rules in a relatively confined space.

Your Turn

Create a Micro-TTRPG of your own. As you'll see, one of the biggest constraints is space. Your game needs to fit in the following pages, so be concise!

Some common elements you may want to include:

- **Character Creation:** Allow the player to specify their own character, within constraints. They can use dice to choose attributes randomly or make them up or create some combination. It may help to prompt them to draw their character.
- **Random Events:** Force players to roll dice and consult a table to determine an event, but allow players to choose how they'll respond to those events.
- **Pass the Baton:** Don't force any one player, or even the game-master, to monologue for too long. Allow players to take over for each other in a helpful way.
- **Reward Players with Freedom:** Allow players to have moments of free-form storytelling as a treat.

TTRPG Name:

Introductory Text:

Characters

Character Sketch

Name:

Attributes:

Character Sketch

Name:

Attributes:

Character Sketch

Name:

Attributes:

Character Sketch

Name:

Attributes:

Event Tables:

1	
2	
3	
4	
5	
6	

1	
2	
3	
4	
5	
6	

Description:

Randomized Game Idea: Roll and Move

Use the dice in the margins to randomly select one of the boxes from each grid. Combine the ideas from each chosen box into a game, and use the following pages to specify that game in as much detail as you can.

	A Dice	**B** Pieces	**C** Movement	**D** Winning
•	Roll one six-sided dice.	Each player has one token; they must move it the number of spaces rolled.	The path has many shortcuts, but players need to land on them exactly to use them.	The first player to reach all five victory spaces wins.
••	Roll two six-sided dice.	Each player has one token; they can move it up to the number of spaces rolled.	When a token moves into the same space as another token from a different player, the other token moves back 10 spaces.	The first player to have visited every space on the cyclical board wins.
•••	Roll two six-sided dice and choose one.	Each player has two tokens, and they must divvy up the number rolled between them.	If a token lands on one of the sad trombone spaces, that token moves back five spaces.	The first player with one of their tokens at the exit wins.
•• ••	Start by rolling four six-sided dice and choosing one. Keep the rest aside. Each turn, roll one new dice and choose a roll from your "hand."	Each player starts with zero tokens. It costs X to add a token and Y to move a token one space.	If an opponent's token is on the same space as yours, you can spend your roll moving your token forward or theirs back.	The first player with all of their tokens at the exit wins.
•• • ••	Roll two six-sided dice. If they match, keep both. Otherwise choose one.	Each player has one token. They can move it the number rolled, or twice, or half.	Every token your token jumps over must move backward one space.	The first player with one of their tokens at the exit loses.
•• •• ••	Roll six six-sided dice under a cup. Before you lift the cup, choose a number between 1 and 6. If any dice match your chosen number, keep them.	Players start with four tokens. All tokens are assigned a number and move only when that number is rolled.	A token cannot move past the token ahead of it unless a certain number is rolled.	The first player with all of their tokens at the exit loses.

Additional rules will be required to make sense of your game. Fill them in here:

_____

_____

_____

_____

Remember to use dice rolls sequentially, and cross out used dice to save your place. Use the following space to sketch out a rough layout of your game board and tokens, and use the following page to formalize your layout, adding interesting spaces connected in a logical way.

Prior Art

There are a lot of roll-and-move games in the world, from the basics like Backgammon, Parcheesi, and Snakes and Ladders to more modern entries like Monopoly and Trivial Pursuit, both of which include a lot of player decision-making. Do you like the purity of rolling and moving, or do you think players need more mechanics to hold their interest?

Cross-Training: Pub Trivia

Trivia is a fascinating subgenre of game, as it literally tests your knowledge, rather than your decision-making, aptitude, or ability. Wagering or category-choice is often added to increase the amount of decision-making required, but fundamentally trivia is about the facts you know, or can figure out. That last part is what makes pub trivia stand out among trivia games. You can figure it out.

Like all trivia, pub trivia requires some background knowledge, but pub trivia also creates opportunities for discussion and collaboration.

Standard Trivia:

Who was the second President of the United States?
(Answer: John Adams)

Pub Trivia:

Which US President was the main character of a popular theatrical production, had one relative who was also president, and had another relative in the beverage industry?

(Answer: John Adams)

Notice that the Pub Trivia question can be approached from multiple angles by teammates well-versed in history, theater, or beer.

Standard Trivia:

In what city was the film *Angels in the Outfield* set?
(Answer: Anaheim, California)

Pub Trivia:

Between 1993 and 1997, three films were made about children who become part of Major League Baseball teams. All three teams still exist today. Name at least two of the three featured Major League Baseball teams.
(Answer: Angels, Cubs, Twins)

Standard Trivia:

What year did Elvis release the song "Heartbreak Hotel"?
(Answer: 1956)

Pub Trivia:

In what year did the following events occur?
- Little Richard releases the song "Tutti Frutti."
- The Winter Olympics are hosted by Italy.
- The first solar-powered radios are sold.
- Future actor Mel Gibson is born.

(Answer: 1956)

The best pub trivia questions involve relating information from many different fields of human endeavor to synthesize a single answer or list of answers.

YOUR TURN

Take the following standard trivia questions and use them as inspiration for your own pub trivia questions.

Standard Trivia:

Who once said "No one goes there anymore; it's too crowded"?
(Answer: Yogi Berra)

Pub Trivia:

Standard Trivia:

What is the shoe industry's term for the plastic cylinder that binds the end of a standard shoelace?
(Answer: Aglet)

Pub Trivia:

Standard Trivia:

The Imperial unit "inch" is based on what older unit of length (which is still used for US shoe sizes)?
(Answer: Barleycorn)

Pub Trivia:

Standard Trivia:

In what year was presliced bread first sold?
(Answer: 1928)

Pub Trivia:

_____
_____
_____
_____

Standard Trivia:

Which months were added to the calendar during the reign of Julius Caesar?
(Answer: July and August)

Pub Trivia:

_____
_____
_____
_____

Standard Trivia:

What country's English name starts with a K and ends with a T?
(Answer: Kuwait)

Pub Trivia:

_____
_____
_____
_____

Now that you've got the hang of adapting standard trivia questions into pub trivia, try writing some from scratch:

_____
_____
_____
_____
_____
_____
_____

Chapter Eight

Bonus Round

———

Golden rule of level design: finish your first level last.

—John Romero

Reflection: Sources of Value in Games

Why do we play games? Some games can be a huge investment of money and time. Even the games that ask the least of their players require their time, attention, and effort. So why do we do it? The scientific explanation is that humans (and many other animals) evolved a psychological drive to play in order to learn and practice the skills they'll need. That said, most of our play has progressed beyond the rehearsal of survival skills.

There is a framework for player motivation developed by the market research firm Quantic Foundry that outlines six key factors: Action (the visceral excitement of play), Social, Mastery (strategic thinking), Achievement (progression and completion), Immersion (including story), and Creativity. Theme park designers separate guest motivation more simply by the "Head" (intellectual interest), the "Heart" (aspirational attraction), and the "Stomach" (the visceral/sensory anticipation).

Game developers are always looking for new ways to deliver value to their players. What is it about games that sparks joy for you? What kinds of value do you enjoy giving to others? How will you make games that honor the investment that players give in return?

Cross-Training: Wireframes

Wireframes are a tool used by graphic designers, user interface designers, and designers from many other fields. They are a skeletal visual representation of the functional elements of a product. Wireframes typically describe situations where a user is interfacing with a screen. They're a great way to visually explain an interactive idea and are thus very useful to game designers as well.

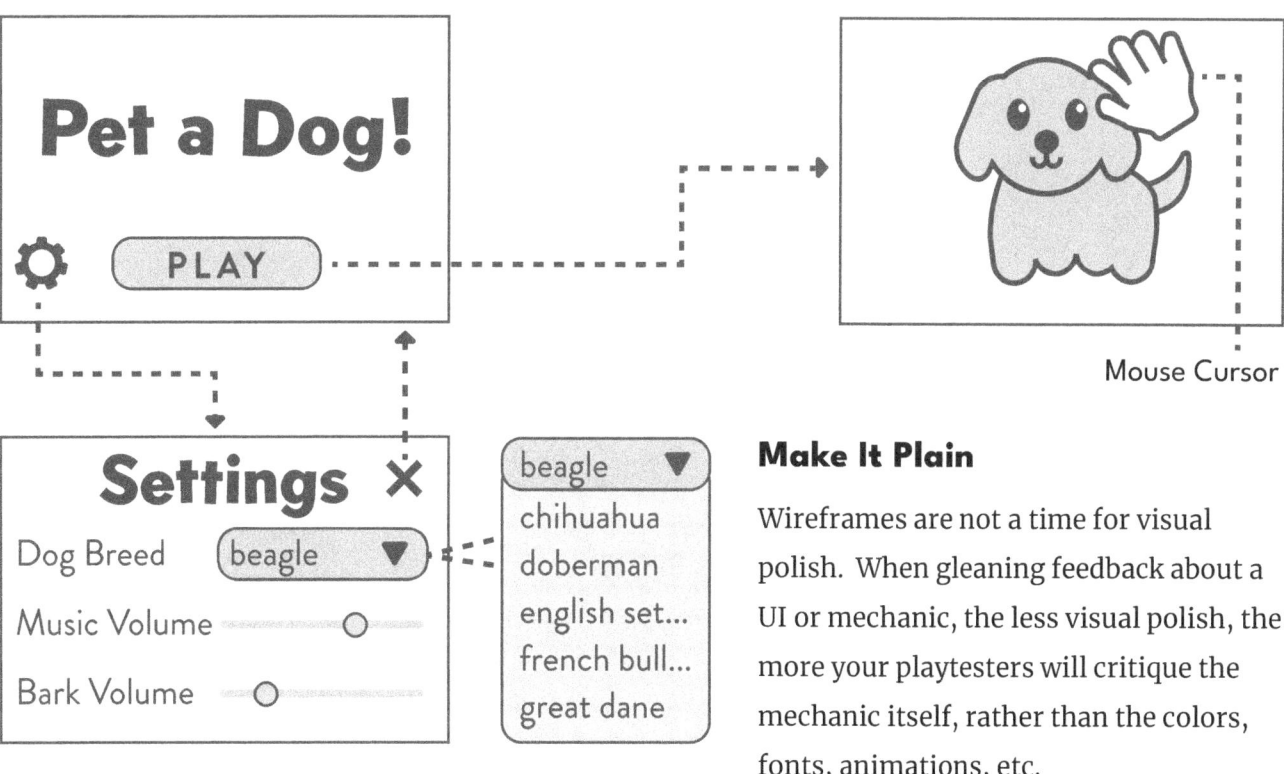

Mouse Cursor

Make It Plain

Wireframes are not a time for visual polish. When gleaning feedback about a UI or mechanic, the less visual polish, the more your playtesters will critique the mechanic itself, rather than the colors, fonts, animations, etc.

Be Specific

Do everything you can to make your wireframes speak for themselves. Having to interject saying "This copy will go here" or "Imagine this image here" makes it harder for people to understand the mechanic.

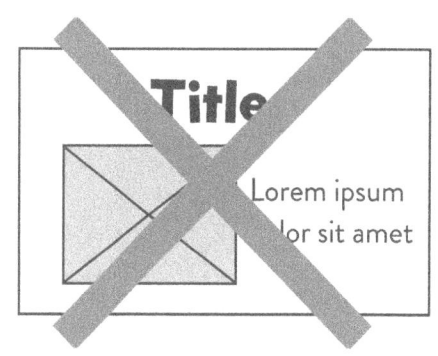

YOUR TURN

Create a wireframe for a simple phone game. It should be a music performance game like Guitar Hero or Rock Band, but using the touch screen. Players should be able to select a difficulty, select a song, adjust volume within the game, and share their scores on social media. Screen templates are provided here with the correct aspect ratio for the target device.

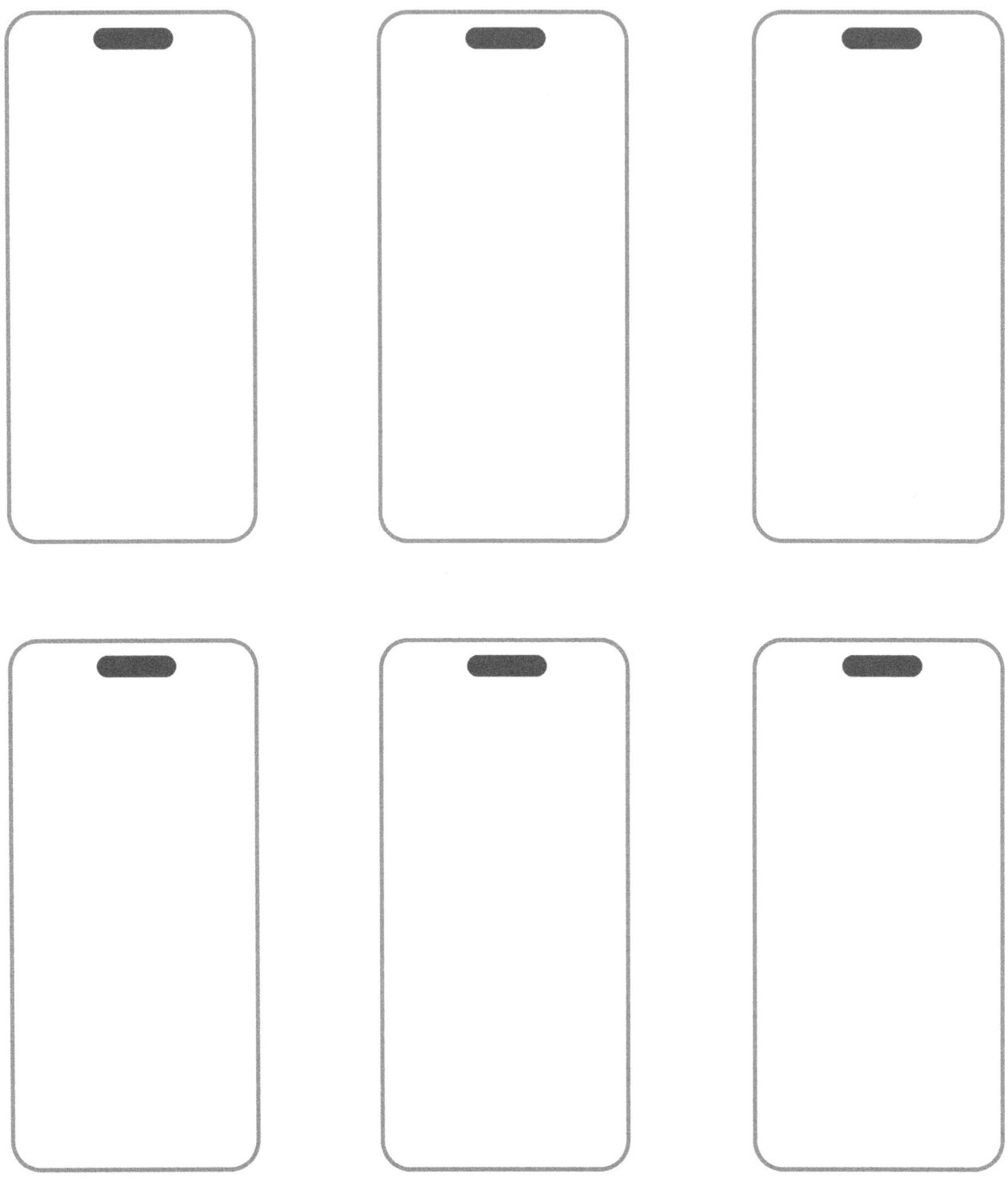

Breaking It Down: Drawing Games

Let's analyze the class of party games that involve conveying information by drawing. The most famous is, of course, Pictionary.

- Only one artist at a time.
- Two teams.
- Choose a random prompt from a pool.
- Reveal the prompt category to all players.
- Draw in public—show the process.
- All teammates attempt to guess the prompt.

Compare this to another popular drawing game, Picture Telephone.

- Everyone plays cooperatively.
- Every player is sometimes an artist.
- Players make up a first prompt.
- Pass the prompt to the next player, who is now an artist.
- Draw the given prompt in private.
- Pass the drawing to another player.
- The player who receives the drawing attempts to guess the prompt.
- The guesser writes their guess.
- The guess becomes the next prompt.
- Repeat the process N times.

For a third example, let's break down the elements of the digital drawing game Drawful by Jackbox Games.

- Every player for themselves.
- Every player is sometimes an artist.
- Players are given a random prompt by the game.
- Draw the given prompt in private.
- Each drawing is captioned by each player.
- Every drawing is shown alongside all player captions, with the original prompt mixed in.

- Players must guess which was the original prompt.
- Points are awarded for guessing correctly.
- Points are awarded if another player incorrectly chooses your caption.

You can see how Drawful has a few elements in common with Picture Telephone. Let's salvage one last example for its useful parts. *A Fake Artist Goes to New York* by Jun Sasaki:

- The "fake artist" and the "question master" are on one team; all other players are on another.
- The "question master" player chooses a prompt.
- Reveal the prompt category to all players.
- The prompt is shown to all players except one, the "fake artist."
- Players take turns drawing a single stroke of a drawing to portray the prompt.
- Players try to guess who is the "fake artist."
- Points are awarded to the player team for successfully identifying the "fake artist."
- Points are awarded to the "fake artist" and the "question master" if the fake artist is not identified.

LET'S BREAK IT DOWN

Do you know another drawing game? If so, break it down into its elements here:

PUTTING IT BACK TOGETHER

Recombine at least three of the elements identified in the previous pages into a new drawing party game, either analog or digital. Add as many new elements as you need to form the result into a coherent game. Outline your new game here (and don't forget to give it a name).

Level Design: Sokoban

Sokoban is a genre of 2D puzzle games about pushing blocks. Even if you've never heard the word, you've probably encountered some kind of puzzle involving pushing a series of blocks that was inspired by sokoban. The constraints are:

Avatars cannot move through blocks.

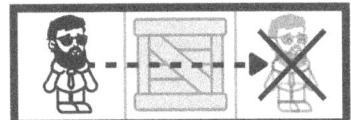

Avatars cannot push more than one block.

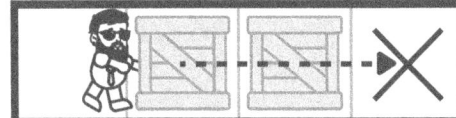

Blocks only move by being pushed from behind.

Sometimes avatars and blocks are allowed to move freely within the walls of the level. Other implementations snap avatars and blocks to a grid. For our purposes let's assume the blocks move only from grid space to adjacent grid space in any cardinal direction.

Get the avatar to the exit and you win!

Here's a simple sokoban puzzle:

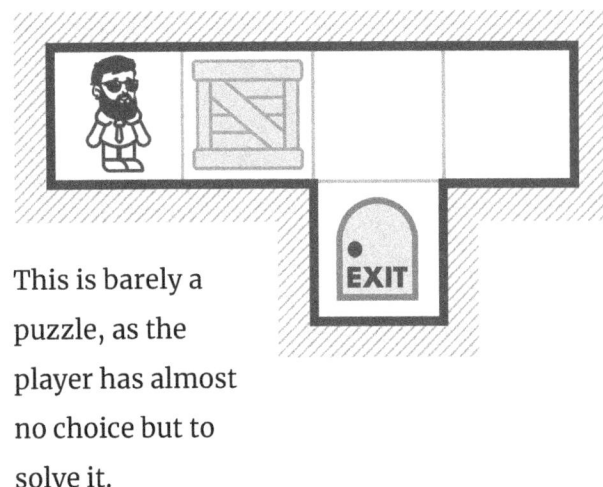

This is barely a puzzle, as the player has almost no choice but to solve it.

This one is a tiny bit harder:

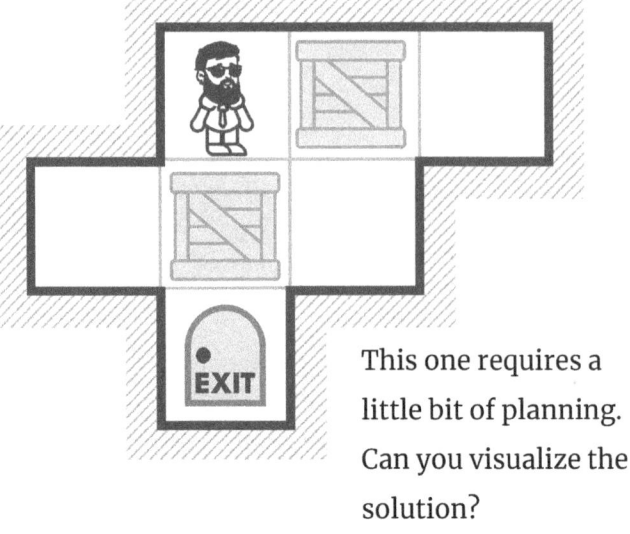

This one requires a little bit of planning. Can you visualize the solution?

More of the same:

This one requires a few more steps but the same number of blocks.

Puzzles should of course include at least one solution and at least one way to get stuck.

YOUR TURN

Try making your own sokoban puzzles with three blocks here:

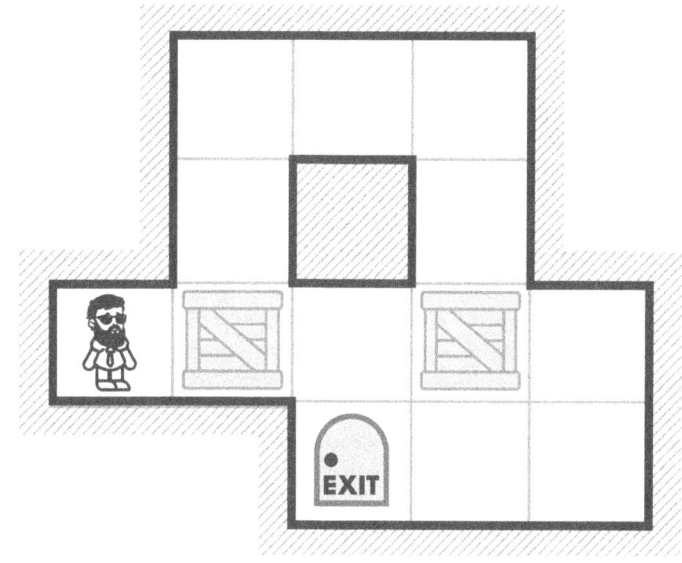

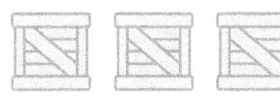

Many implementations of sokoban add new kinds of blocks, for instance, key blocks. Locks are stationary and prevent avatars from moving through them, but when a key block touches a lock, both disappear. In every other way, key blocks behave like an ordinary block.

As you can see, this creates further puzzle possibilities.

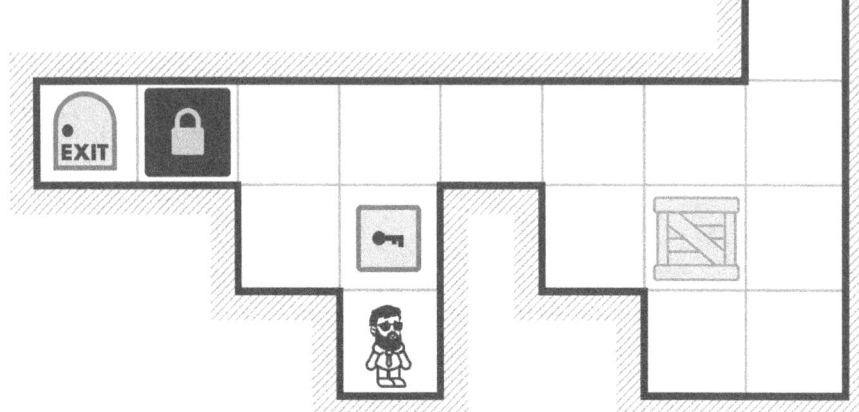

YOUR TURN

Make your own sokoban puzzle with a key block, a lock, and two normal blocks here. Remember, your level doesn't need to use the space frugally. You may want to add more space than is necessary to misdirect the player (but be careful that you don't accidentally create a more direct solution in the process).

What about two keys and
two locks?

This is more interesting to
solve but also harder
to design.

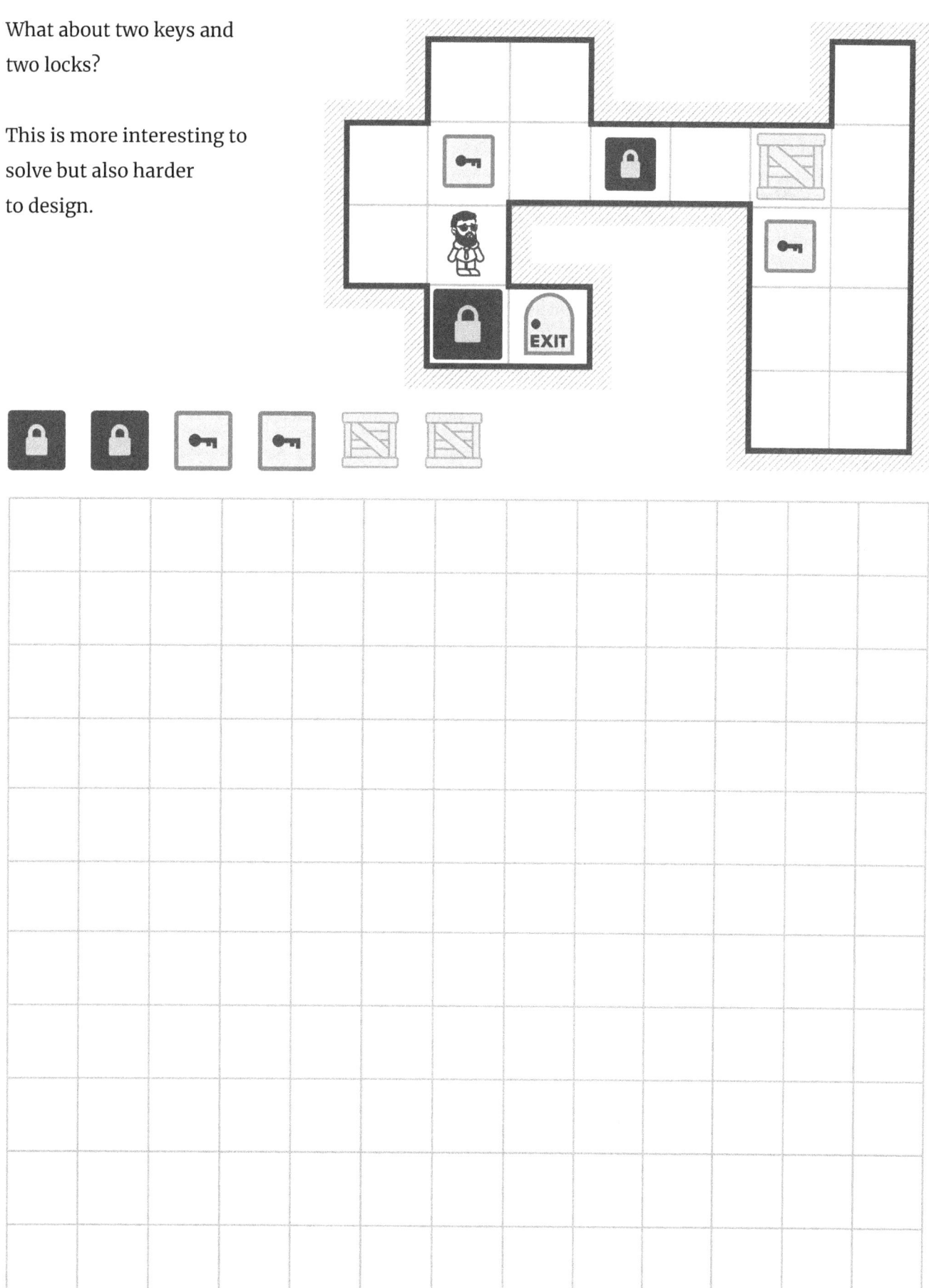

Reflection: Continuing to Grow

As we reach the end of this book, it's only natural to begin to think about how you'll continue to improve your game design skills and intuition. Whether you're a student or working professional in the field it's easy to find your game design practice deepening without broadening. Ideally, you should find a way to continue to grow, and in an uncommon direction if possible. It's your unique set of influences and abilities that make you, and your games, stand out in a crowded domain. So how do you plan to stay sharp and to develop your distinctive voice?

Further Reading

This book, and our practice of game design, draws on the previous work of many others, including the authors listed in the following pages. Check them out to learn more!

Chapter 1: Setting the Stage

Reflection: Who Is the Game Designer You?
- *Honoring the Code: Conversations With Great Game Designers* by Matt Barton
- *Postmortems* by Raph Koster
- *Blood, Sweat, and Pixels* by Jason Schreier

What Is...a GDD?
- *Zach-Like: A Game Design History* by Zach Barth

Remix: Tic-Tac-Toe (Naughts & Crosses)
- *The Rules We Break* by Eric Zimmerman

Level Design: Mazes
- *Mazes in Videogames: Meaning, Metaphor and Design* by Alison Gazzard
- *The Art of the Maze* by Adrian Fisher and Georg Gerster

What a Concept: Accessibility
- *Accessibility for Everyone* by Laura Kalbag
- *The Field Guide to Human-Centered Design* by IDEO.org

Cross-Training: Schematic Drawing
- *101 Things I Learned in Architecture School* by Matthew Frederick

Breaking It Down: Capturing the Feeling
- *Game Feel* by Steve Swink

Randomized Game Idea: Pencil-and-Paper Games
- *Pentagames* by Pentagram

Chapter 2: Abstract Strategy

Reflection: A Gameplay Memory
- *Breakout: Pilgrim in the Microworld* by David Sudnow

Remix: Connect Four
- *The White Box Essays* by Jeremy Holcomb

What a Concept: Forks
- *My 60 Memorable Games* by Bobby Fischer

Level Design: Dots and Boxes
- *The Art of Game Design: A Book of Lenses* by Jesse Schell

What Is...MDA?

- *Elements of Game Design* by Robert Zubek

Narrative Design: Abstract Strategy

- *Procedural Storytelling in Game Design* by Tanya X. Short and Tarn Adams

Breaking It Down: Discretizing Time and Space

- *Rules of Play: Game Design Fundamentals* by Katie Salen and Eric Zimmerman
- *Game Mechanics: Advanced Game Design* by Ernest Adams and Joris Dormans

Narrative Design: Theming

- *Slay the Dragon: Writing Great Videogames* by Robert Denton Bryant & Keith Giglio

Randomized Game Idea: Abstract Strategy

- *Characteristics of Games* by George Skaff Elias, Richard Garfield, and Robert Gutschera

Chapter 3: Story

Cross-Training: Storyboarding

- *Storyboarding Essentials* by David Harland Rousseau and Benjamin Reid Phillips

What a Concept: Story Flow

- *Twisty Little Passages: An Approach to Interactive Fiction* by Nick Montfort

Narrative Design: Roll and Move

- *Quests* by Jeff Howard

Randomized Game Idea: Hidden Role

- *Building Blocks of Tabletop Game Design: An Encyclopedia of Mechanisms* by Geoffrey Engelstein and Isaac Shalev

Breaking It Down: Anatomy of a Story

- *Morphology of the Folktale* by Vladimir Propp
- *The Hero with a Thousand Faces* by Joseph Campbell

Chapter 4: Sport

Reflection: Rules Heavy and Light

- *Homo Ludens: A Study of the Play-Element in Culture* by Johan Huizinga

Remix: Basketball

- *The Way To Play: The Illustrated Encyclopedia of the Games of the World* by The Diagram Group

Randomized Game Idea: Sport

- *Challenges for Game Designers* by Brenda Brathwaite and Ian Schreiber

Breaking It Down: Playground Games

- *The Well-Played Game: A Player's Philosophy* by Bernard DeKoven

Cross-Training: Toy Design
- *A World Without Reality: Inside Marvin Glass's Toy Vault* by Bill Paxton
- *Wham-O Super Book* by Tim Walsh

Chapter 5: Word Games

Reflection: Serious Games
- *What Video Games Have to Teach Us About Learning and Literacy* by James Paul Gee
- *Making Games for Impact* by Kurt Squire
- *Making Deep Games* by Doris C. Rusch

Remix: Word Scramble
- *How to Play SCRABBLE Like a Champion* by Joel Wapnick

Level Design: Crossword Puzzle
- *Will Shortz Picks His Favorite Puzzles: 101 of the Top Crosswords from The New York Times* by Will Shortz

What a Concept: Chain Reactions
- *A Game Design Vocabulary* by Anna Anthropy and Naomi Clark

Chapter 6: Quantitative

Reflection: Player Feedback
- *Playful Design: Creating Game Experiences in Everyday Interfaces* by John Ferrara
- *The Philosophy of Design* by Glenn Parsons

What a Concept: Emergence
- *A New Kind of Science* by Stephen Wolfram

Breaking It Down: Balance
- *Game Balance* by Ian Schreiber and Brenda Romero

What a Concept: Randomness
- *Clockwork Game Design* by Keith Burgun
- *Uncertainty in Games* by Greg Costikyan

Narrative Design: Variables
- *Make Your Own Twine Games!* by Anna Anthropy

Level Design: Race Track
- *Level Up! The Guide to Great Video Game Design* by Scott Rogers

Remix: Battling Ships
- *Game Design Workshop: A Playcentric Approach to Creating Innovative Games* by Tracy Fullerton

Chapter 7: Outside the Box

Reflection: Player Creativity

- *Lifelong Kindergarten: Cultivating Creativity Through Projects, Passion, Peers, and Play* by Mitchel Resnick
- *The Imagineering Workout* by The Disney Imagineers

Cross-Training: Theme Park Design

- *Theme Park Design & the Art of Themed Entertainment* by David Younger
- *Marc Davis in His Own Words: Imagineering the Disney Theme Parks* by Pete Docter and Chistopher Merritt

Breaking It Down: Bodies

- *The Infinite Playground: A Player's Guide to Imagination* by Bernard DeKoven and Holly Gramazio

Narrative Design: Micro-RPG

- *The Ultimate Micro-RPG Book* by James D'Amato

Randomized Game Idea: Roll and Move

- *Your Turn!! The Guide to Great Tabletop Game Design* by Scott Rogers

Chapter 8: Bonus Round

Reflection: Sources of Value in Games

- *Rise of the Videogame Zinesters: How Freaks, Normals, Amateurs, Artists, Dreamers, Dropouts, Queers, Housewives, and People Like You Are Taking Back an Art Form* by Anna Anthropy

What a Concept: Randomness 2

- *Advanced Game Design: A Systems Approach* by Michael Sellers

Cross-Training: Wireframes

- *Universal Principles of Design* by William Lidwell, Kritina Holden, and Jill Butler
- *Creative Workshop: 80 Challenges to Sharpen Your Design Skills* by David Sherwin

Breaking It Down: Drawing Games

- *The Gamer's Brain* by Celia Hodent

Level Design: Sokoban

- *An Architectural Approach to Level Design* by Christopher W. Totten

Appendix A: Random Dice, Cards, Letters

Letters		Dice		Scrabble				Cards				Cards			
D	D	4	1	T¹	S¹	E¹	U¹	A	6	6	9	A	6	K	6
A	B	4	4	E¹	N¹	T¹	L¹	5	2	4	3	7	9	A	3
C	B	4	3	P³	I²	E¹	D²	Q	10	8	K	10	8	A	7
D	B	2	3	F⁴	D²	B³	V⁴	K	8	Q	7	3	A	10	5
C	C	4	1	S¹	E¹	R¹	R¹	J	J	7	8	8	J	8	Q
D	B	1	4	U¹	H⁴	O¹	R¹	3	10	6	K	2	9	6	9
B	D	2	1	A¹	I¹	G²	T¹	2	5	J	5	J	K	5	9
D	D	2	3	L¹	L¹	M³	W⁴	8	K	A	7	8	3	5	2
C	B	3	3	A¹	V⁴	C³	N¹	7	A	6	5	Q	K	7	4
B	C	2	4	N¹	I²	Y⁴	S¹	3	4	3	Q	4	10	4	J
A	C	1	4	A¹	O¹	N¹	O¹	9	9	2	Q	6	Q	5	7
A	A	3	2	T¹	A¹	E¹	A¹	10	A	10	9	Q	J	2	3
B	C	2	3	G²	M³	N¹	D²	2	4	4	J	10	K	4	2
A	A	1	1	K⁵	O¹	R¹	J⁶								
A	A	1	4	B³	O¹	C³	E¹								
B	D	3	2	H⁴	I²	L¹	I²								
B	B	1	2	G²	D²	P³	I²								
A	B	4	1	J⁶	A¹	R¹	F⁴								
C	C	3	2												
A	A	3	3												
D	C	2	4												
C	A														
B	A														
A	C														
D	B														
A	B														
D	B														
C	D														
C	D														
D	A														

Appendix B: Additional Workspaces and Grids